Roller Hockey

The Game Within the Game

D1596329

Roller Hockey

The Game Within the Game

A Player and Coach Handbook

Warren R. Taylor

Gabriel Publications

Typography: Synergistic Data Systems
Cover design: Dale Schroeder, SDS, sdsdesign@altrionet.com

Publisher: Gabriel Publications, Sherman Oaks, California 91423, (800) 940-2622, www.GabrielBooks.com

Library of Congress 2001092137

ISBN 1891689-82-7

This book is dedicated with all my love to my roller hockey family: my wife Sue, my two sons David and Warren Jr., my daughter-in-law Lynn, and to my grandsons Jacob and Zachary.

Contents

Chapter 7:

Chapter 8:

Chapter 9:

Chapter 10:

Chapter 11:

Appendix A:

Appendix B: Favorite Practice Drills

Appendix C:

List of Illustrations

Foreword

Dave Cairns
Canada National Team Coach

*I*n 1993 the creation of the first professional roller hockey league, Roller Hockey International, marked the acceptance of this sport throughout the world. Since this date the sport has continued to grow at a fast pace even though limited by the lack of playing facilities and the scarcity of relevant roller hockey knowledge.

In the past few years the rate of construction of roller hockey facilities has increased substantially as a result of improved designs and lower costs. The scarcity of roller hockey knowledge remains as the last vital ingredient that is still needed to sustain and accelerate the continued growth and development of this exciting sport.

Beginning coaches may have sufficient knowledge to be able to focus on their own teams. More proficient coaches armed with more knowledge are able to focus on their opponents. The most effective coaches are able to focus, analyze, and communicate the tactics, playing styles, and interactions of both teams. They are the innovators who possess both the knowledge and the understanding of the essential elements of this sport.

Roller hockey programs around the world strive to accelerate the development of their coaches as well as their players through these three phases or levels described above. I am sure that **Roller Hockey: The Game Within the Game,** will be a vital tool that can be used for this purpose.

With a unique flow and writing style, **Roller Hockey: The Game Within the Game** provides all the fundamental knowledge of roller hockey that every coach and player needs to have. Its main premise is that the rink the players must use is much different from the rink the spectators see. This innovative concept is the foundation that enables every reader to rapidly gain a clear understanding of the "game within the game" that is played on the "rink within the rink".

I strongly recommend **Roller Hockey: The Game Within the Game** as required reading to roller hockey coaches and players around the world. It will empower coaches and players at any level with the confidence, competence, and passion to continue to advanced levels in this sport.

About Dave Cairns

Dave Cairns was born in Winnipeg, Manitoba, Canada on September 10th, 1964. At the age of 5 years he strapped on his first pair of skates and began to play ice hockey. Originally as a goaltender, his hockey career led him through high school, junior league play in the neighboring province of Saskatchewan, and then on to the University of Manitoba.

After graduation he continued to play as a professional in Switzerland and later as a coach in England, Switzerland, and Denmark. When a severe automobile injury ended his professional ice hockey playing career in 1992 he returned to Canada.

With the creation of the first professional roller hockey league, Roller Hockey International in 1993, he began his involvement in the sport of roller hockey. In the first year of league operations he became Player/Assistant Coach of the RHI VooDoo in Vancouver, British Columbia, Canada. In 1994 Dave became Head Coach of the RHI VooDoo and led them to consecutive Conference Championships through 1997.

In 1997, Dave coached the Canadian National Roller Hockey Team to a silver medal in the world championships. In 1998 this team won the gold medal.

In 1999, Dave moved to Buffalo, New York as the Player/Head Coach of the RHI Buffalo Wings. When RHI ceased operations in 1999 he was their most successful coach having accumulated the most wins in RHI history.

Shortly thereafter Dave relocated to Southern California. Currently Dave is a facility and development consultant with Sportcite Management Group in Orange County, California.

Dave has developed and continues to operate the largest club level roller hockey program in North America at various roller hockey rinks in this area. He continues to conduct roller hockey clinics for coaches and players throughout the world.

Introduction

Mike Doers
RHI All Star Player

Roller hockey is a sport that continues to grow throughout the world at a rapid pace. There is a great demand for modeling basic elements of this sport in order to facilitate the continuous and progressive skills development of its players, coaches, and officials. I believe that **Roller Hockey: The Game Within the Game** will aid and accelerate this process.

Many other roller hockey publications contain plays, diagrams, and drills, which stress *what* to do. This book will describe the concepts of this sport from an insider's perspective, stressing *why* to do the actions that will enhance your motivation to play, coach, or watch as a fan.

As I read **Roller Hockey: The Game Within the Game**, I learned some things that I didn't know and some new ways to explain things that I hadn't ever thought of. Warren's section on dividing the rink floor into zones and providing rules and strategies for each zone is invaluable. His player's rink concept and team-play discussion are the most valuable portions of the book and set it apart from all others.

I commend Warren for providing a much needed manual specifically for roller hockey. His material will help everyone to understand roller hockey concepts in a very short period of time. He has included an excellent basic understanding of the game for beginners as well as material that will aid experienced coaches, players, parents, and fans.

If you are a roller hockey player, there are valuable lessons in each section of **Roller Hockey: The Game Within the Game** that will help you to learn and practice skills to take your game to the next level. If you are a roller hockey coach, you will find play diagrams and descriptions that will help you teach the game of roller hockey to your players more effectively. If you are a roller hockey spectator and fan, the insights in this book will allow you to deepen your understanding and passion for this exciting sport.

About Mike Doers

Mike Doers was born in Madison, Wisconsin on June 6th, 1971. At the age of 3 years he strapped on his first pair of skates and began to play ice hockey. His hockey career led him through Northwood Prep high school, to his freshman college year at the University of Vermont in Burlington Vermont, and then on to the University of Wisconsin in Madison, Wisconsin for his final three years of college.

In 1988 Mike was drafted by the Toronto Maple Leafs in the 6th round and named to the USA Select 18 Team. In 1990 Mike was selected for the USA Junior Olympic Team.

After graduation from university in 1994 he continued to play ice hockey as a professional in the East Coast Hockey League with the Dayton Bombers in Dayton, Ohio. Soon after the creation of the first professional roller hockey league, Roller Hockey International (RHI) in 1993, he began his involvement in the sport of roller hockey.

In the summer of 1994, Mike was recruited to try out for the Los Angeles Blades entry in the RHI league and was selected as a player. Mike played as a professional for the Los Angeles Blades from 1994 through 1996 and was selected for the 1995 RHI Western Conference All Star Team.

In 1997, when the Los Angeles Blades and the RHI professional league ceased operations, he turned his attention to coaching and teaching, first with RHI Amateur until 1998 and then with DK Hockey until 1999, holding clinics and teaching seminars throughout the western United States.

In 1999 he joined the Team Express in Huntington Beach, California as a professional in the newly formed Professional Beach Hockey league. He was a major contributor helping the Team Express to winning seasons in 1999 and 2000, as well as the PBH Championship in 1999.

In 1999, Mike was also recruited to join Coast2Coast Inline Hockey in Huntington Beach, California. As the Hockey Director for this organization, Mike has developed and operated the largest club and recreational level roller hockey program in North America.

Mike and his wife Cindy live in the Southern California area. He continues to conduct roller hockey clinics for coaches and players throughout the area.

Acknowledgments

*F*or the reader, acknowledgment pages can be pretty boring stuff. However each name represents an important contributor to this book whom it would be totally unfair to overlook:

Mike Doers, Inline Hockey Director at Coast 2 Coast In-Line Hockey Center in Huntington Beach gave me my first opportunity to coach roller hockey in the Spring of 1999. You have continued to provide expert review of this material, advice, and much encouragement over the last three years. I will be forever indebted to you.

Brian Waterfield, dedicated Toronto Maple Leafs Hockey fan, and walking compendium of hockey trivia and knowledge in Toronto Ontario provided needed guidance and historical data on the origins of the sport of hockey.Thanks for being my friend and northern hockey lifeline.

Bob Bayer, roller hockey coach, player, and avid Los Angeles Kings fan in Huntington Beach provided review, advice and encouragement in the initial development of this material. Your insights and guidance were invaluable.

Bill and Debbie Leisy, avid roller hockey parents and fans in Long Beach provided the impetus to gather this material into book form and encouraged me to publish it. Your encouragement and assistance will always be greatly appreciated.

Marko Peers, roller hockey coach and motivator extra-ordinaire in Mission Viejo reviewed and utilized much of this material with many of his roller hockey teams to ensure its validity and application. Thank you for your friendship, active participation and encouragement.

Jeff Andrews, avid roller hockey parent and assistant coach in Huntington Beach provided review and encouragement combined with unique parental perspectives that helped me to maintain a clear focus for this material. Thank you for your friendship and support.

Clive Gillon, roller hockey coach, fan, and player at The Cooler in Alpharetta Georgia provided expert and analytical editing of many of my draft versions. Your contributions and recommendations added to the clarity, accuracy, and material content of the final version. Thank you for your continued friendship, support and expert advice.

About the Author

Warren Taylor was born in St. Catharines, Ontario, Canada and strapped on his first pair of ice skates at the age of three. His father introduced him to the game of ice hockey when he magically created a hockey rink in his backyard one cold winter evening. A hockey stick, a few hard rubber pucks from the local Canadian Tire outlet, and a makeshift goal followed in a matter of days. Soon every afternoon after school he could be found playing a game most Canadians know as "shinny" on this backyard rink with his neighborhood friends.

At the age of six his father took him to the Garden City Arena to watch his first game of organized hockey on an artificial ice surface. The magic of that day ignited a passion in him for the sport of hockey that changed his life.

Soon thereafter Warren began to participate in organized youth ice hockey leagues offered at that arena and continued to do so through high school. He attended Cornell University on a hockey scholarship, and after graduation from Cornell he went to work in the computer industry in the midwestern United States. Although career and family commanded most of his attention and time, he continued to play hockey on a limited basis through adult league play and occasional late-night pick-up games with his friends at local rinks.

Many years later, after relocation to Southern California and at the urging of his youngest son, David, he strapped on his first pair of roller skates. Soon he found himself playing street hockey in front of his home on weekends with his family and the neighborhood children. It didn't take long for his passion for ice hockey to be redirected. In 1998, when his son David wanted to play organized roller hockey at a local rink, he volunteered to be a coach in this program. Warren has been coaching and teaching roller hockey ever since.

In order to accelerate the development of his players, Warren began to develop coaching notes, diagrams, and innovative practice drills which he shared with his players, their parents, and fellow coaches each season. These notes and diagrams have been brought to publication in this book through the urging of many of Warren's players, their parents, as well as his fellow coaches. Players, parents, and coaches alike have found that this book allowed them to gain an understanding of roller hockey basics—the "game within the game" that is played on "the rink within the rink".

Today Warren lives with his wife, Sue, and their son, David, in Southern California. He continues to coach and teach roller hockey in the Southern California Area.

1
How to Use This Book

*T*his book is organized to allow the reader to quickly and easily gain a good understanding of the basic fundamentals of the sport of roller hockey.

The foundation upon which this book is based is the concept that the rink as utilized by the players and coaches is different than the rink as seen by spectators and fans. This "rink within the rink" contains areas and territory definitions that are not marked on the rink surface for everyone to see. In each of these areas there are individual player skills as well as team skills that must be learned and practiced to be successful. It is in these areas that the players must play the "game within the game".

The chapters of this book will provide a flow of information that can be taken to the practice rink and dressing room a chapter at a time. Each subsequent chapter builds upon information and concepts described in the previous chapters.

Chapter 1: How to Use This Book

Provides a description of each chapter and appendix in this book with recommendations on how to best use the information it contains.

Chapter 2: The Spectators' Roller Hockey Rink

Describes the playing surface that the spectators see with its offensive and defensive end zones, the face-off circles and dots, as well as the goal and its protective crease area.

Chapter 3: The Players' Roller Hockey Rink

Describes the playing surface that the players must see and utilize effectively with its three playing lanes, the central red line zone or transition area, the slot area, and the defensive curtain.

Chapter 4: Team Play Concepts

Introduces and describes the basic concepts of team play: offense, defense, and the importance of advancing the puck forward into your opponent's territory at every opportunity.

Chapter 1

Chapter 5: Team Skills I

Introduces four fundamental team skills that must be learned: how to move or "double" the puck out of the defensive end; how to defend the middle lane and slot area in the defensive end; how to attack the middle lane and slot area in the offensive end; and how to control and maintain possession of the puck in the opponents end zone.

Chapter 6: Team Skills II

Adds a fifth vital team skill that must be learned: how to master a face-off both in the offensive and defensive end zones with special emphasis on team positioning when the face-off is won and lost in both zones.

Chapter 7: Team Skills III

Adds the sixth and last vital team skill that must be learned: how to optimize team positioning and defensive play to effectively kill penalties when they result in a manpower advantage for the opposing team.

Chapter 8: Player Skills I

Introduces the primary individual skill that must be learned first by every player: how to play defensively with special emphasis on defensive positioning on the rink surface and checking an opponent to regain possession of the puck.

Chapter 9: Player Skills II

Adds the individual offensive skills that must be learned: how to combine the skills of stickhandling, passing, and skating to create effective offensive plays.

Chapter 10: Player Skills III

Provides information that will enhance a player's ability to shoot the puck and score goals with special emphasis on optimum shooting targets, different goaltender net minding styles, rink locations that offer the best scoring opportunities, and recommended types of shots to utilize.

Chapter 11: Player Skills IV

Insights into the art and skills of goaltending with special emphasis on positioning for optimum coverage of the net and reducing the shooters shot angle to the net.

Appendix A: Coaches Corner: Player Quicktips

Offers a summary of one or two line "quicktips" that can be easily remembered or memorized by coaches and players as the lessons in this book are taken to the practice rink and to competitive game contests.

Appendix B: Favorite Practice Drills

Outlines a few favorite practice drills that the author has found to be effective in the teaching and learning of these team and individual skills. These practice drills can form the "starter set" for a comprehensive practice drill library that the reader can continue to build over time.

Appendix C: Parent Fan Stands

Is a special supplement for parents and family fans. Included are sections describing roller hockey program orientation, recommended player equipment, player and parent/fan code of conduct, practice session objectives and intent, playing time conventions and expectations, and recommended team communication methods as well as some sample forms that may be utilized for this purpose.

The chapters of this book provide the basis of an integrated lesson plan for coaches and players who are eager to learn, teach, and enhance their roller hockey skills. Delivery of this information on a regular weekly basis to players and parent/fans will provide the foundation for a continuous, accelerated learning system for roller hockey coaches and players.

Access to this information can be facilitated using a website that will distribute this information as weekly player study notes. An example of such an approach can be found at *http://www.rollerhockeycoach.com*, a website initially developed and published by the author to support his own roller hockey coaching activities in Southern California. You are invited to dial in and skate through this site at your convenience.

2
The Spectators' Roller Hockey Rink

*T*he standard roller hockey rink that the spectators and fans see is shown in Figure 2.1. The center red line divides the playing surface on this rink into two equal halves—one half is the defensive end for each team or the end where that team's goal is located. The other half is the offensive end for each team or the end where the opponent's goal is located.

Figure 2.1 The Spectators' Roller Hockey Rink

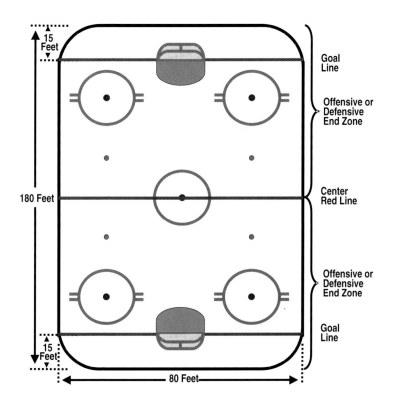

As shown in Figure 2.1, the standard roller hockey rink measures 180 feet long and 80 feet wide with rounded corners. This surface will be enclosed with vertical boards and netting or clear polyethylene plastic to a height that will allow the puck to remain within the playing surface. This rink design promotes a continuous flow of play while protecting spectators and fans from being hit by errant pucks.

This rink will have a goal net centered in each end zone that defines a goal line 15 feet from the end boards. These goal nets define a rectangular box shaped scoring area. As shown in Figure 2.2, the front vertical plane of this rectangular box-shaped scoring area is 6 feet wide and 4 feet high. As shown in Figure 2.3, the depth of this box-shaped scoring area is approximately 2 feet at the top and 3 feet at the base. The rear plane of this box shaped scoring area is supported in the center by a vertical back brace post.

Figure 2.2 The Standard Roller Hockey Goal (Front View)

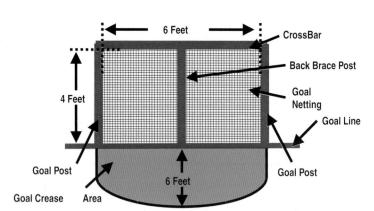

The back and sides of this rectangular box shaped scoring area are enclosed with heavy duty nylon netting to catch and retain the puck within this rectangular box-shaped scoring area once it has crossed the front vertical plane. The line across the top of this front vertical plane is known as the cross bar while the connecting vertical lines are known as the goal posts. The line across the base of this front vertical plane is the goal line.

The entire* puck *must cross the goal line for a goal to be scored.

Figure 2.3 The Standard Roller Hockey Goal (Side View)

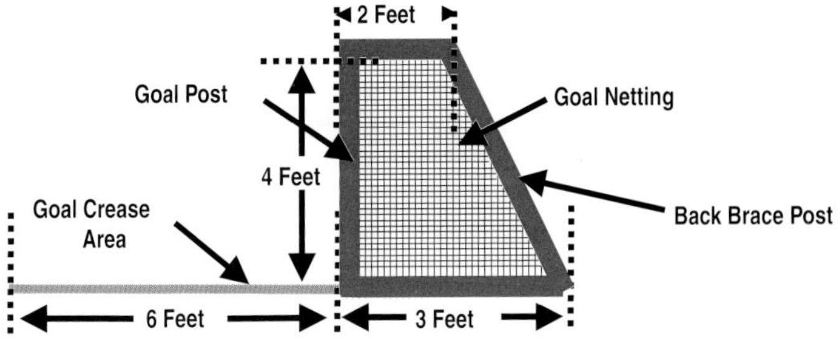

The circular rounded area on the rink surface in front of each goal is the goal crease area. This area measures 6 feet in diameter from the goal line at its furthest point. No player other than the goaltender is allowed to occupy this area under normal circumstances. An offensive player is only allowed to enter this area in pursuit of the puck that is not in the possession of the goaltender. This means that the puck must enter this area before any offensive player.

The goal crease area is intended to provide a safety zone for each goaltender that will decrease his chance for injury. Inside this area an offensive player cannot physically touch or otherwise hamper the goaltender in his efforts to prevent a goal from being scored. This area also defines a buffer zone directly in front of each goal that is intended to provide the goaltender with an unhampered view of the puck when it is shot toward the goal.

The puck is allowed to move at will anywhere on the rink surface without regard to player positioning. This rink design promotes a continuous flow of team play with very few stoppages.

Stoppages in play can occur for a variety of reasons. Play is resumed after a stoppage using a face-off at one of the face-off circles or dots marked on the rink surface.

There are five large red circles on the rink surface with smaller filled-in red circles or dots in the middle of each circle. These are the standard face-off circles. The face-off circle on the center red line is used to initiate play at the start of each period of play and after each goal has been scored. The remaining four face-off circles are utilized to resume play after a stoppage. There are four additional face-off dots that have no surrounding circles located on either side of the center red line. These can also be utilized to resume play after a stoppage.

In a face-off, each team will line up on their defensive end side of the face-off dot. Each team will present one player at this dot that will contend for possession of the puck. Each of these face-off contenders will face each other with their hockey sticks outside of the dot area. All other players must remain outside of the face-off circle area or at a distance indicated by the game official. As shown in Figure 2.4, a game official will drop the puck fairly between these players at the center of the face-off dot.

Figure 2.4 Roller Hockey Face-off

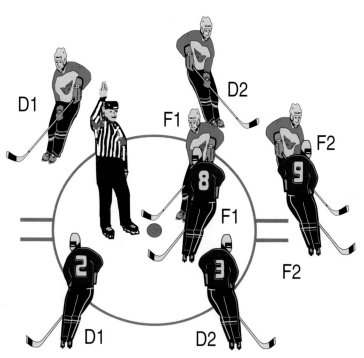

Each roller hockey team will consist of 5 players. As shown in Figure 2.5, each team will play a two-man forward line (forwards F1 and F2) and a two-man defense line (defenseman D1 and D2) unless penalized. Each team will also play a goaltender.

Figure 2.5 Roller Hockey Team Player Assignments

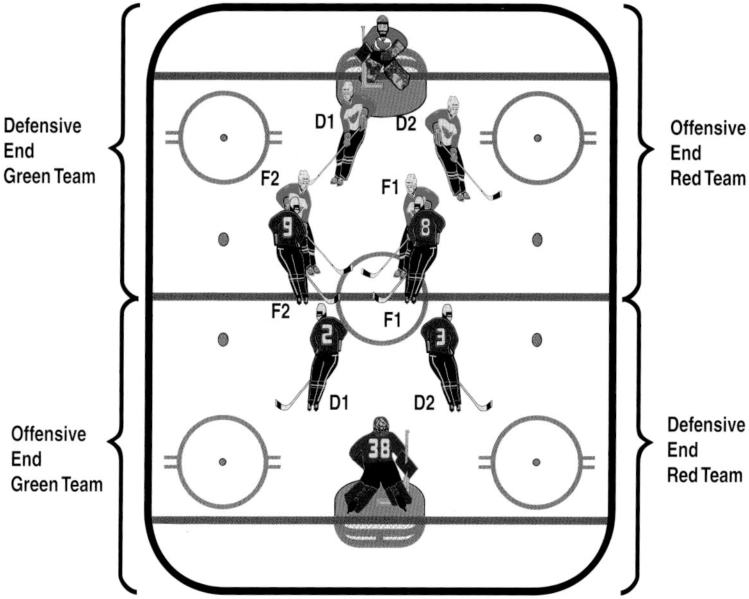
Defensive
End
Green Team
Offensive
End
Red Team
D1
D2
F2
F1
F2
F1
D1
D2
Offensive
End
Green Team
Defensive
End
Red Team

3

The Players' Roller Hockey Rink

*T*he standard roller hockey rink that the spectators see is not the rink that the players must see. The rink that the player's must see is different. As shown in Figure 3.1, this rink, as viewed by a player, will include the center red line, the goal lines, and all the *face-off* circles that the spectators see. It will also include areas of the playing surface that are not marked visibly with lines or circles. It is these areas and the control of play in these areas by each team that will determine most game outcomes. These invisible areas include the "*slot*", the "*defensive curtain*", the three "*playing lanes*", and the "*transition area*".

Figure 3.1 The Players' Roller Hockey Rink

11

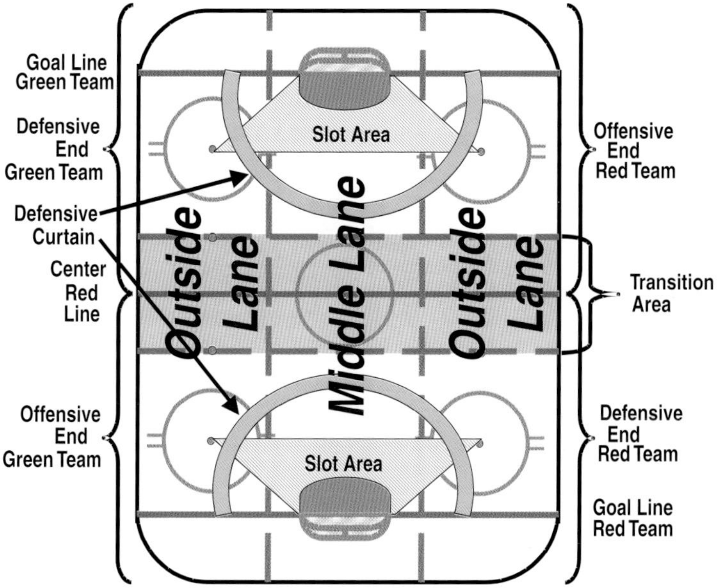

The Three Playing Lanes

From a player's perspective, the playing surface is separated end-to-end into three lanes of equal width. These lanes are imaginary and are not marked on the playing surface. As shown in Figure 3.2, there is one middle lane situated between two outside playing lanes. For best results players and the puck will flow back and forth between only two adjacent playing lanes as the puck is moved up and down the rink—the center lane and one of the outside lanes.

Control of the puck in the center or middle lane is most important and will determine the outcome of most hockey games. As shown in Figure 3.2, the Green Team in their defensive end should always attempt to keep the puck in one of the outside lanes and out of the middle lane in their defensive end of the rink. This is to ensure that if a mistake is made, the opposition team will not gain control of the puck directly in front of their goal with the best chance of quickly getting to the slot area.

Figure 3.2 The Three Playing Lanes

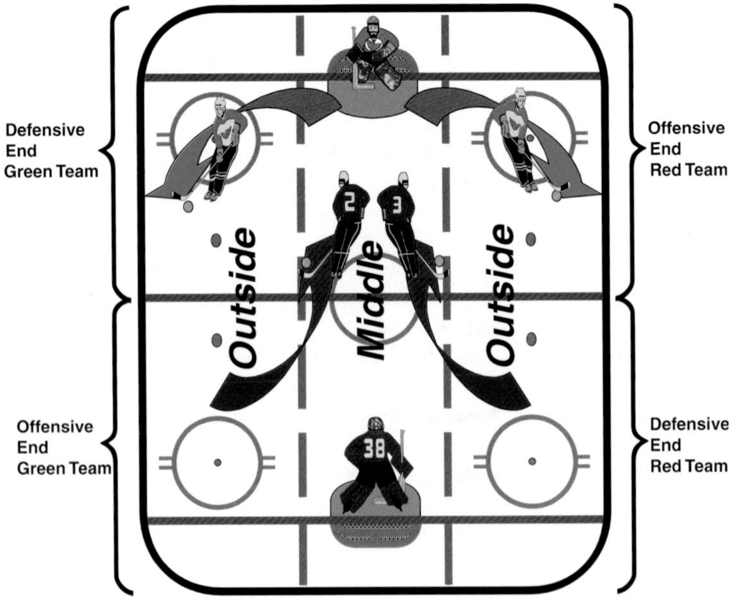

Conversely, as shown in Figure 3.2, the Red Team has taken the puck over the center red line into their offensive end and should always try to move the puck into the area directly in front of their opponent's goal in the center lane. It is from this area that most goals will be scored.

The Transition Area

The transition area stretches from side-to-side on both sides of the center red line. As shown in Figure 3.3, it occupies the area between the face-off dots on either side of the center red line. Teams will use this area to complete the transition of play from defense to offense and conversely from offense to defense.

Figure 3.3 The Transition Area

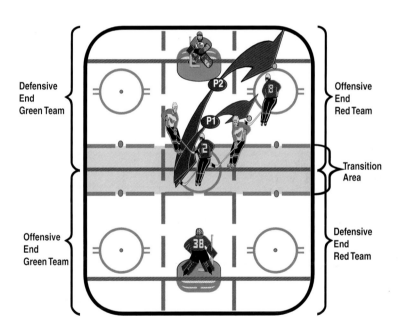

The transition area is a danger zone. Turnovers in this area usually result in a reversal of puck direction that causes a significant man advantage and scoring opportunity for the other team. Attempting to stickhandle past defending opponent players in this area is the most common cause of these turnovers. When opponent players are present in this area, it is important to advance the puck quickly into the offensive end. The first priority is to get the puck over the center red line into your opponent's defensive end zone. Make a forward pass **[P1]** across the red line to a teammate or shoot the puck **[P2]** into the opponent's end and then chase it to regain possession.

The line at center is painted red for a good reason—danger lurks near this line!

When no other option is available, dump the puck across the red line into your opponent's end. If you turn over possession of the puck at or near the center red line, you will usually give a scoring opportunity to your opponents!

The Slot

The slot is the most active area on the playing surface. It is an area bounded by the two face-off centers and the goal posts in each end of the rink that extends out in front of the goal. It is an

Figure 3.4 The Slot Area In The Offensive End

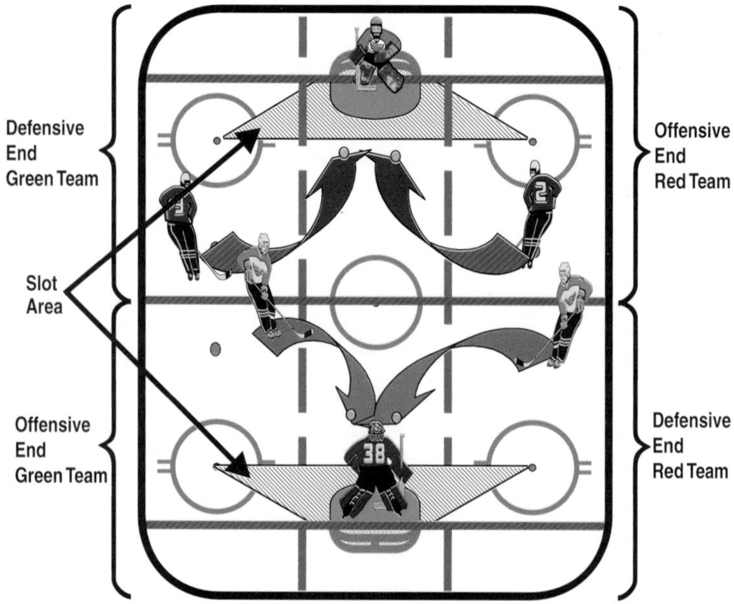

imaginary area and is not marked on the playing surface. As shown in Figure 3.4, it is the area shaded in red in front of each goal.

This is the most effective offensive area from which to shoot and to score. For this reason the slot is the prime target area to get the puck to in the opponent's end.

As shown in Figure 3.4, once an offensive player has crossed the center red line into his offensive end with the puck in his possession, he should attempt to move the puck into the middle lane in order to attack the slot area.

An offensive player should always attempt to shoot, advance, or pass the puck into the slot area in his offensive end.

Conversely the slot area is the most dangerous area to allow the puck to get to in your defensive end.

A defensive player should always attempt to remove the puck from the slot area in the defensive end. This means that he should not attempt to stickhandle or skate with the puck in this

Figure 3.5 *The Slot Area In The Defensive End*

15

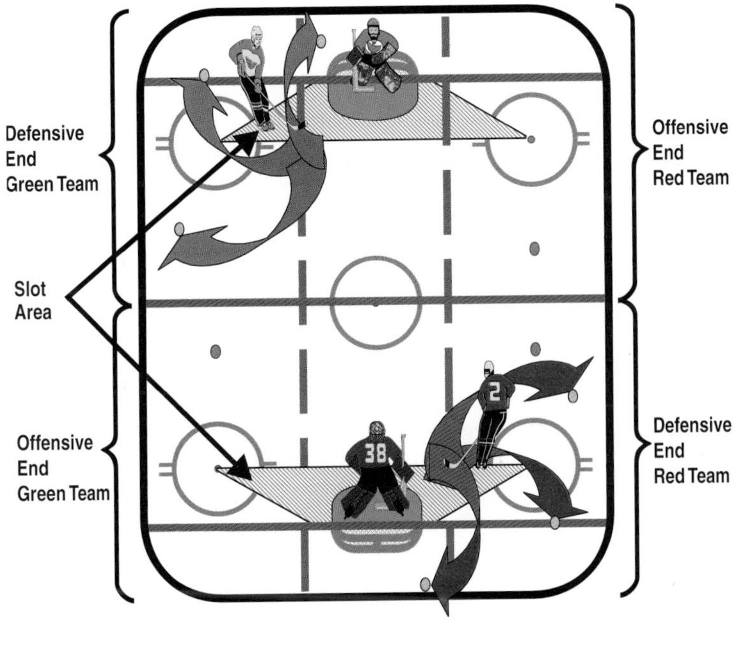

area. In addition he should never attempt to clear, advance, or pass the puck to one of his teammates through the slot area in his defensive end.

As shown in Figure 3.5, a defensive player should first always attempt to clear the puck from the slot area by slapping or shooting the puck behind his goal or to the side of his goal to one of the outside lanes.

Once the puck has been cleared from the slot area, a defensive player can then advance the puck by skating with it, passing it to one of his teammates, or simply shooting it against the boards out of his end zone.

A defensive player should always attempt to clear or remove the puck from the slot area before he attempts to advance or pass the puck to one of his teammates.

The Defensive Curtain

The defensive curtain is not marked on the playing surface. As shown in Figure 3.6, it is a gold curtain or wall that extends in a semi-circle around and in front of the slot area. Good defen-

Figure 3.6 The Defensive Curtain

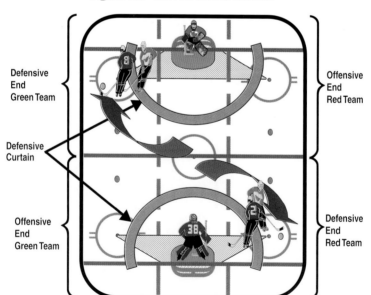

sive play is to never let the puck be brought past this curtain into the slot area by the offensive team.

Good defensive play will begin to challenge the puck carrier as soon as he has reached the top of the face-off circle and attempt to take away his control of the puck. Good defensive play does not mandate that the puck carrier is checked resulting in a change of puck possession. Good defensive play can also include making the puck carrier pass or shoot the puck before he really wants to do so.

In all circumstances good defensive play will always force the player with the puck to one of the outside lanes away from the middle lane and the slot. Good defensive play should only allow the player with the puck to attempt to shoot on goal from the other side of this imaginary curtain—to the side and a long distance away from the goal. Such shots are low percentage shots and should be easily seen and stopped by most goalies.

4

Team Play Concepts

*A*ll players are encouraged to participate in team offense and team defense. Players who excel at this are admired as *"two-way players"*. Forwards must play defensively when control of the puck is lost to an opponent. Defensemen must play offensively when control of the puck has been accomplished.
   Offense and defense are team responsibilities!

Team Offense

Offense is a prime responsibility of all players. Forwards are expected to gain and maintain control of the puck in their offensive end as well as to forecheck when they lose control of the puck in their offensive end. Defensemen are also expected to advance the puck offensively at all times. Once the puck has been advanced into the opponent's defensive end, defensemen are expected to position themselves there as well (inside the red line) in order to actively participate in all offensive plays.
   As shown in Figure 4.1, Green Team defensemen D1 and D2 have positioned themselves inside the Red Team's defensive end and are ready to pass and receive the puck from their forward teammates F1 and F2.

Advancing the Puck

All players are also encouraged to advance the puck out of their defensive end at every opportunity. This involves moving the puck quickly up the rink towards your opponent's goal. Rapid forward movement of the puck makes the puck do the work and your opponents do most of the skating. This is called *"tipping the rink surface"*.
   Roller hockey is a game of mistakes that transition into offensive opportunities. When the majority of play can be sustained in your opponent's defensive end, defensive mistakes made by your opponent can quickly and easily be turned into scoring opportunities for your team. At the same time, mistakes you make in your opponent's defensive end are a long way from your own goal and can usually be overcome.
   In order of priority, the best ways to advance the puck through and past opponent players are:

Figure 4.1 Offensive Team Positioning

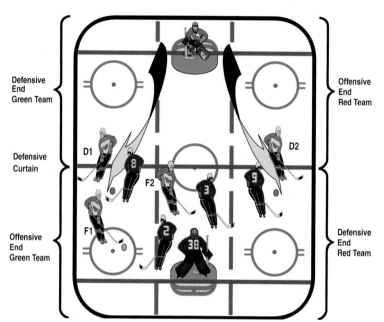

1. passing the puck forward to a teammate so that possession of the puck is maintained,

2. shooting the puck forward towards the opponent's defensive end (commonly referred to as dumping the puck) and then chasing it quickly to regain possession of the puck, and

3. skating forward with possession of the puck attempting to stickhandle past all defending opponent players.

The most effective way to advance the puck is to pass the puck forward to a teammate!

Quick forward passes make your opponents stop their forward motion and transition to defense. Rapid stopping, turning, reversing direction, and skating backwards will tire your opponents not you. Most mistakes are made when fatigue sets in. Keeping your opponents "on their heels" will also have a psychological effect. By the third period of the game you will have plenty of gas left in your tank—your opponents won't.

Don't skate with the puck unless you have to! Take a look to find a teammate up the rink and pass him the puck! Keep the puck moving forward! A two stride limit is strongly recommended. Take no more than two strides with the puck then pass it to one of your team mates.

Once you have gained possession of the puck in your opponent's end it is important to keep the puck moving and in play. Again the most effective way to do this is to pass the puck to an open teammate. Always look for the open man wherever he might be and give him the puck.

It is also important not to give the opponent goaltender a chance to catch or smother the puck when you release a shot on net. When no open scoring hole is available to shoot at, don't blast away at his glove area or directly at his midsection. Hit the net with your shot - shoot the puck low at the goaltender's pads so that a rebound occurs. This might provide your teammate a chance to score instead. More importantly this will keep the puck moving and in play.

Team Defense

Defense is the first responsibility of all players. Defensemen are expected to gain and maintain control the puck especially in the defensive end.

However, forward players are also expected to contribute to team defense. When your opponents have control of the puck in your defensive end, forwards are expected to "**backcheck**". This means that once control of the puck has been lost to an opponent, forwards are expected to skate back into their own defensive end to help their own defensemen regain control of the puck. A forward's first responsibility should always be to deny an opponent access to the center lane and the slot. Trying to check an opponent player off the puck should always come second.

As shown in Figure 4.2, Red Team forwards F1 and F2 have skated back into their own defensive end and positioned themselves to defend shots on goal or passes involving the Green Team defensemen. If needed, they are also positioned to assist the Red Team defensemen D1 and D2 to regain control of the puck.

Figure 4.2 Defensive Team Positioning

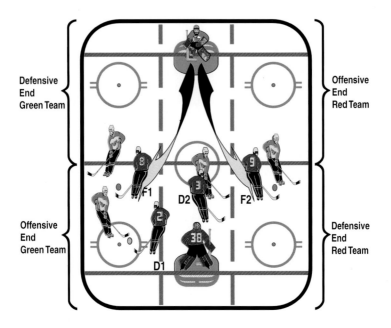

Defensive
End
Green Team

Offensive
End
Red Team

Offensive
End
Green Team

Defensive
End
Red Team

5
Team Skills I

Doubling the Puck Out of Your End

"Doubling the puck*" out of your end allows the puck to be moved out of your defensive end zone utilizing two short, quick passes. This can also be accomplished using the boards to assist the movement of the puck whenever necessary. This play requires the defensive team forwards to skate back into their own defensive end and position themselves to receive or give an *"outlet"* or *"breakout"* pass.

As shown in Figure 5.1, one Red Team defenseman D1 has gained control of the puck in his defensive end. The other Red Team defenseman D2 has positioned himself in front of his net

Figure 5.1 The Double Out Play

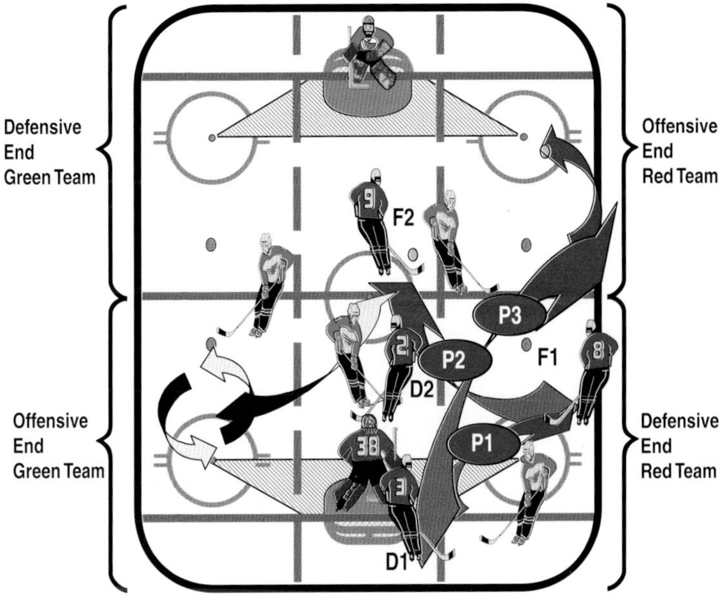

Defensive End Green Team

Offensive End Red Team

Offensive End Green Team

Defensive End Red Team

to protect his goalie and to clear any errant passes that might come his way.

As a general rule, when the puck is in your end, the first player back should retrieve the puck, the second player back should always position himself in front of his net to check an opponent forward or to clear any pucks that enter the slot area. The third player back should go to the boards on the puck side of the rink and position himself to receive the first outlet pass. The fourth or last player back should go to the other outside lane and circle back and inward to receive the second outlet pass.

One Red Team forward player F1 has positioned himself in the outside lane nearest the defenseman D1 who has control of the puck. This Red Team forward player F1 has positioned himself with his back to the boards and his stick on the rink surface between the top edge of the nearest face-off circle and the center red line. The Red Team defenseman D1 with the puck should attempt to make the initial outlet pass **[P1]** to the Red Team forward F1.

As shown in Figure 5.1, the remaining Red Team forward F2 has rushed forward up the center lane between the Green Team defensemen for a *"breakaway"* pass **[P2]**. Initially he positioned himself in open territory inside the center red line and in position to receive an outlet pass. Red Team forward F2 circled in a continuous motion from the outside lane back towards his goalie and inward toward the center lane. Circling in this fashion allowed Red Team forward F2 to check the Green Team defenseman D1 in the event his Red Team could not maintain possession of the puck. More importantly this circling allowed Red Team forward F2 to accelerate quickly into and up the center lane.

These two quick or double passes give this play its name.

If an outlet pass to the Red Team forward F1 cannot be made safely, the Red Team defenseman D1 with the puck should attempt to clear the puck **[P3]** out of his defensive end. Clearing the puck should be attempted as quickly as possible by shooting the puck up along and against the boards in the outside lane—*never the middle lane.*

Clearing the puck can also be used as an attempt to pass the puck to the other Red Team forward F2 by shooting the puck with enough speed to send it across the red line deep into the opponents' end. This allows Red Team forward F2 to chase the

puck into the offensive end and re-gain possession. This is called
"***dumping***" the puck into the opponent's end.

As a last resort the Red Team defenseman D1 can skate out
with the puck if there are no opponent players directly in his way.

***Never under any circumstances should the center or
middle lane be used in your defensive end zone except to gain
control of the puck.***

Use of the boards to assist movement of the puck is encouraged. Bouncing the puck off the boards at an angle is the same as
passing the puck to one of your teammates and having him
advance it forward.

Every attempt must be made to quickly advance the puck forward out of your defensive end—to transition as quickly as possible from defense to offense in order to try to gain an odd-man
advantage going the other direction.

Another variation of this play provides a "***give-and-go***" of
the puck between the Red Team defenseman D1 with the puck
and the Red Team forward F1. In this variation the Red Team
defenseman D1 originates an outlet pass **[P1]** to his Red Team
forward F1 using one of the outside lanes.

Figure 5.2 The Give-and-Go Double Out Play

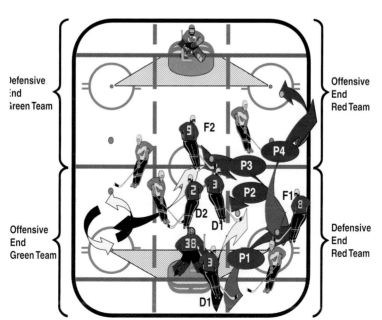

As shown in Figure 5.2, Red Team defenseman D1 then continues to skate forward towards the opponent's goal staying within this same outside lane and quickly receives a return forward pass **[P2]** from the defensive forward F1.

Defenseman D1 will now advance the puck into the opponent's end as quickly as possible by:

1. passing the puck **[P3]** ahead to his Red Team forward linemate F2, or

2. shooting the puck **[P4]** against the boards into the opponent's end.

These two quick or double passes give this play its name.

Attacking the Middle Lane

Once a team on offense can cross the center red line with possession of the puck, it should make every attempt to move the puck into the middle lane in the opponent's defensive end. It is from this position that the puck can be advanced into the slot area and a high percentage shot on goal can be attempted.

Figure 5.3 Attacking the Middle Lane

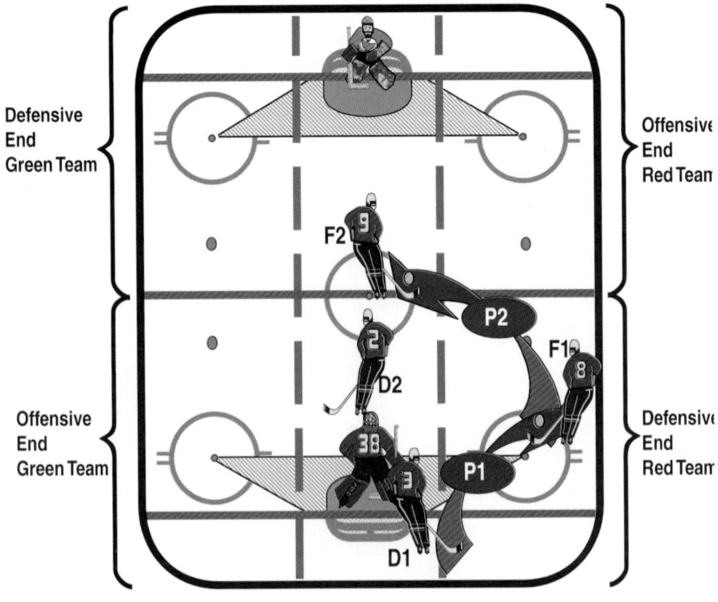

The primary offensive goal is to get the puck into the slot area within the center lane in your opponent's defensive end.

Attacking your opponent's center lane is one of the most difficult strategies in hockey to complete.

One of the best ways to advance the puck out of your defensive end and across the center red line into the opponent's center lane is shown in Figure 5.3. In this example, Red Team Defenseman D1 will pass [P1] the puck to Red Team Forward F1 along the boards in the outside lane. Red Team Forward F1 will advance the puck [P2] to Red Team Forward F2 across the center red line and into the center lane. Red Team Forward F2 will now take the puck to the slot area for a high percentage shot on goal.

Defending the Middle Lane

Effective defensive play will attempt to prevent the movement of the offensive puck carrier into the middle lane. Effective defensive play will only allow the puck or the puck carrier to enter one of the outside lanes in the defensive end of the rink.

Figure 5.4 Defending the Middle Lane

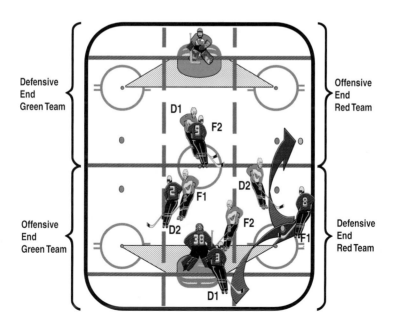

27

As shown in Figure 5.4, defensive Green Team players have positioned themselves accordingly and are attempting to deny the offensive Red Team any access to the center lane. Each defensive Green Team player is positioned to intercept an errant pass or to check his Red Team counterpart when he advances into the center lane area. The only lane that the Red Team can safely use to advance the puck is the right outside lane.

Keep the puck and the puck carrier between you and the boards and away from the center lane—to stay "inside" the puck and the puck carrier.

Don't give up the middle—make your opponent skate wide around you in one of the outside lanes.

Control of the Puck in Your Opponent's End

Hockey, like other team sports, is a game of control. A hockey team must be able to control possession of the puck in an effective manner, especially if it is going to score. When a team has control of the puck it can pass it, skate with it, and shoot it. These are all factors that provide a team with scoring opportunities. Many good scoring opportunities will be generated if control of the puck can be maintained in the opponent's end.

When the puck is in the opponent's end, all members of the offensive team must first position themselves in two adjacent lanes inside their opponent's end. A common mistake made by many teams is to leave one or more of their defensemen on the other side of the red line. This leaves two or three offensive team members and four defensive team members in the defensive end to contest for possession of the puck. This manpower advantage will assist the efforts of the defensive team to regain control of the puck and quickly transition the play back to the offensive team's end.

Optimum player positioning will create a diamond shape with a player at each point of the diamond.

As shown in Figure 5.5, the offensive forward F1 will position himself in the offensive corner in one of the outside lanes. In this illustration offensive forward F1 has possession of the puck. Offensive defenseman D1 will be positioned near the side boards in the same outside lane as offensive forward F1 about five feet inside the center red line. Offensive forward F2 should always be positioned in the slot in front and slightly to the side of the opponent's goaltender. Offensive defenseman D2 will be positioned at the far edge of the center lane just outside the high slot area directly in front of the net.

Figure 5.5 The Offensive Diamond

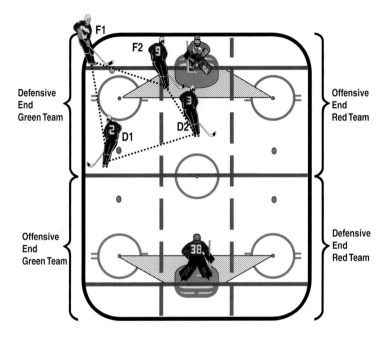

The offensive team should first try to get the puck to the slot area where a high percentage shot on goal can be released. As shown in Figure 5.6, passing the puck **[P1]** to offensive forward F2 in the slot is one way to make this happen. Passing the puck **[P2]** to offensive defenseman D2 who has moved into the high slot area is another very good alternative.

If this is not possible the offensive team should next attempt to spread out the defenders both vertically and horizontally. Spreading out the defenders will make it easier to complete a pass around or by them.

As shown in Figure 5.7, passing the puck **[P3]** back to offensive defenseman D1 at the furthest point of the triangle will spread the defenders vertically.

In order to spread out the defenders horizontally, the puck must be moved to the other outside lane. As shown in Figure 5.8, passing the puck **[P4]** from offensive defenseman D1 to offensive defenseman D2 on the other side of the rink is one way to accomplish this. Passing the puck along the end boards behind

Figure 5.6 Passing to the Slot Area

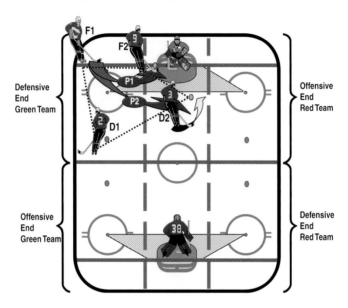

Figure 5.7 Spreading the Defenders Vertically

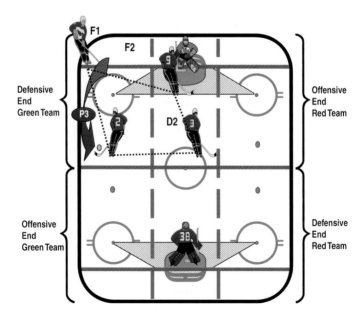

the net **[P5]** to offensive forward F2 in the other offensive corner in the other outside lane is another way to accomplish this.

To spread the defenders horizontally, offensive forward F2 must first move to the corner in the other outside lane to receive the pass along the end boards. After the pass has been released offensive forward F1 must move to take a position in front and slightly to the side of the opponent's goaltender. As you would expect the positions of the offensive defenseman must also switch. Defenseman D2 must move laterally to take a position in the other outside lane near the boards about five feet inside the center red line. Defenseman D1 must also move laterally to take a position at the far edge of the center lane just outside the high slot area directly in front of the net.

As shown in Figure 5.8, note that the diamond shape referenced earlier is still intact but will have shifted to the other side of the rink.

Figure 5.8 Spreading The Defenders Horizontally

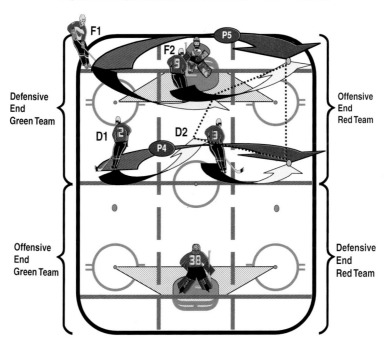

On either side of the rink, it is important that offensive players maintain their relative positioning inside two adjacent lanes inside the opponent's end. A distance of about ten or twelve feet between each offensive player is recommended. If offensive teammates are too close together, one defender will be able to cover both. Conversely if offensive teammates are too far apart, passes between them will be more easily intercepted.

The offensive team must try to keep the defensive team from gaining control of the puck. More importantly this means that the offensive team must never give away possession of the puck or turn it over voluntarily. They must force the defensive team to take it away only if they can . . . to contest and earn every single possession.

One of the most common ways to voluntarily turn over the puck in your opponent's end is to attempt a "blind" pass into the slot area from one of the corners. A blind pass is one that is simply shot into an area without looking first to see if a teammate is open or eligible to receive the pass. Most blind passes end up on a defensive team member's stick and result in a turnover.

As illustrated in Figure 5.9, offensive forward F1 has control of the puck in the corner. If he attempts a blind pass to his offensive forward teammate F2 in the slot area or to offensive defenseman D2 across the slot area, it will most likely be intercepted by one of the defensive players.

It is more effective for offensive forward F1 to keep control of the puck in the corner until the nearest defender comes to challenge him for its possession. This will open up a passing lane to another offensive player.

Control of the puck can be maintained by moving the puck around the outside perimeter until a high percentage shot on net becomes available.

As shown in Figure 5.9, this requires effective and accurate passing **[P1]** from offensive forward F1 to offensive defenseman D1, then **[P2]** on to offensive defenseman D2. If a high percentage shot on net can not be taken from the high slot area, the puck can then be passed **[P3]** to offensive forward F2 who can take the shot on net. If offensive forward F1 can not release a shot on net the puck can be passed **[P4]** to offensive forward F1 in the corner. At this point another "cycle" of the puck can be initiated.

At any point in the "cycle" the flow of the puck can be reversed by immediately returning the puck to the last passer.

Figure 5.9 Using the Perimeter to Control the Puck

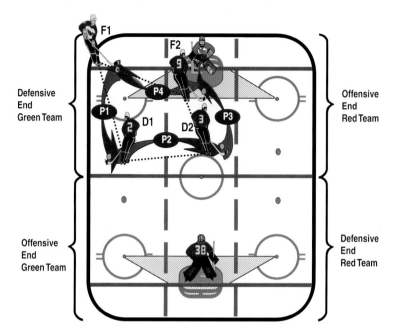

With the receipt of each pass there is the option of immediately shooting on goal if a high percentage shot becomes available. The highest percentage shot on net will come from the slot area. Who takes the shot will depend upon which side of the rink is utilized by the offensive team to "cycle" the puck. This shot can be taken by either of the offensive defenseman who can skate into the slot area to receive a pass or the offensive forward in the slot area.

The best scoring opportunity will usually result from a pass to an offensive defenseman who has skated into the high slot area. Even if his shot is blocked by the goaltender, at least one offensive forward will always be in front of the net for a rebound or to collect the puck and move it to the outside lane so that another "cycle" can be initiated.

It is important to look before you pass to make sure your intended recipient is open and eligible to receive your pass.

Maintain control of the puck—don't give it away voluntarily. Make your opponent work hard to take it away from you.

Have patience, "cycle" the puck to a teammate, and wait for a good high percentage shot on your opponent's goal from the slot area.

Remember to always think defensively—the defenseman on the strong side of the rink (the same side of the rink where the puck is) is the safety valve and should always be the furthest back nearest the center red line.

6

Team Skills II

Face-Off Concepts

*f*ace-offs are utilized to resume play after a stoppage. In a face-off, the referee drops the puck between an offensive and a defensive player in the center of the nearest face-off circle allowing them to contest for its possession. There are five face-off circles: two in both the offensive and defensive ends as well as one at the center red line in the middle of the rink.

Winning a face-off is an art that is difficult to learn and master. Excellent hand/eye coordination in combination with fast reflexes and considerable upper body strength is required.

There are four set plays that can be used by either team in this situation:

1. Draw

2. Flip

3. Shot

4. Block/Steal.

A face-off is not won unless you gain control of the puck. The draw play is the best and preferred play to gain control of the puck.

The draw play allows the puck to be removed from the face-off circle backwards or behind the player taking the face-off.

The flip play allows the puck to be removed from the face-off circle with a short sideways or forward pass to a teammate.

The shot play removes the puck from the playoff circle with a direct shot on goal right from the face-off circle.

The block/steal allows the puck to be removed from the face-off circle by a teammate after the opponent player taking the face-off has been neutralized or blocked from gaining control of the puck.

Once control of the puck has been accomplished, movement of the puck on the rink will depend upon whether the face-off was taken in the offensive or the defensive end.

Chapter 6

Face-Offs in the Offensive End

A team on offense with an offensive end face-off must make
every attempt to move the puck into the middle lane slot area in
order to take a high percentage shot on the opponent's goal.
Lining up correctly to take the face-off is the first and most
important step.

An appropriate lineup is shown in Figure 6.1. In this formation the offensive forward F1 will take the face-off. Offensive
defenseman D1 will be positioned behind forward F1 in the outside lane outside and furthest back from the face-off circle.
Offensive forward F2 should always be positioned on the inside
center lane never along the boards. Offensive defenseman D2
will be positioned outside the face-off circle in the same outside
lane near the top of the slot area.

***Optimum player positioning will create a diamond shape
with a player at each point of the diamond.***

Figure 6.1 Face-off Formation in the Offensive End

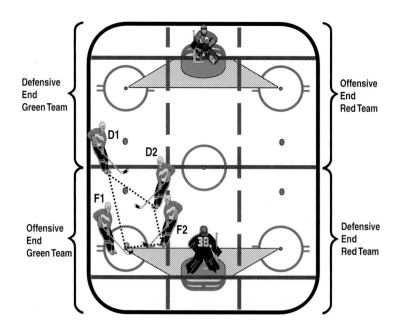

When the Face-Off Is Won in the Offensive End

When the face-off is won, as shown in Figure 6.2, offensive forward F1 will draw the puck back [**P1**] to defenseman D2 and then impede his face-off opponent's progress forward to the puck. Defenseman D2 can now quickly take a high percentage shot [**S1**] on the opponent's goal. If defenseman D2 cannot release his shot on net he can quickly pass [**P2**] back to defenseman D1 who can release a shot [**S2**] on the opponent's goal. Offensive forward F2 will momentarily impede his opposite opponent and then go to the net to screen the goaltender, to deflect the shot from either defensemen, or to score on a rebound after the shot has been taken.

When the offensive forward F1 cannot cleanly draw the puck back he should immediately attempt to tie up his face-off opponent while keeping the puck behind his skates. If possible he can kick the puck back to defenseman D2. Defenseman D2 can also rush forward to retrieve the puck in this case for a shot on net or a pass to defenseman D1 who will release the shot.

Figure 6.2 Winning Face-offs in the Offensive End

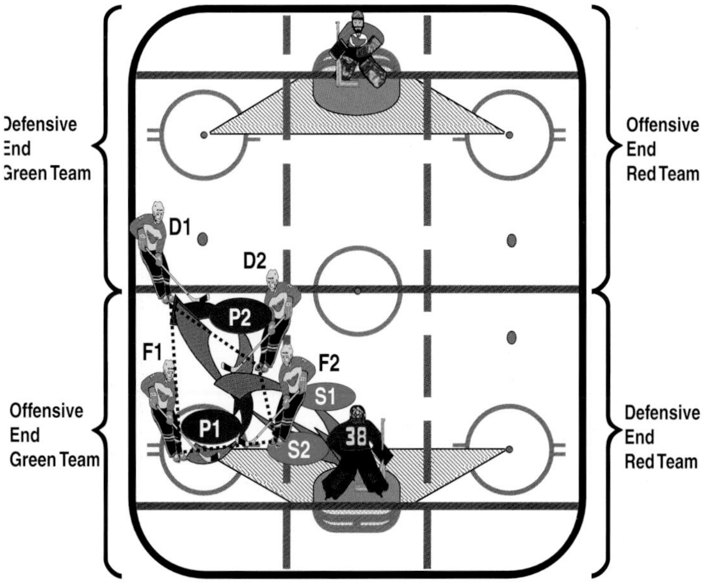

When the Face-Off Is Lost in the Offensive End

When the face-off is lost, each offensive player is still positioned well to check and regain control of the puck. Each offensive player should attempt to restrict the movement of the puck to the outside lane on the same side of the rink that the face-off was taken and lost.

Figure 6.3 Losing Face-offs in the Offensive End

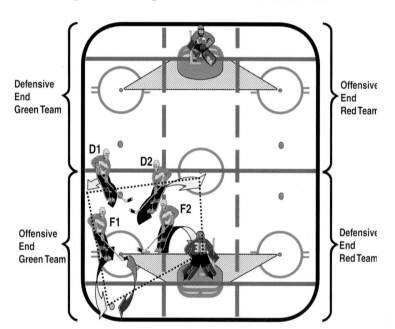

As shown in Figure 6.3, offensive forward F1 should quickly rush forward to put pressure on the opponent with the puck forcing him to the corner nearest the face-off circle. His prime goal should be to force the puck to be cleared against the near sideboards and not cleared behind the net to the other outside lane. Offensive forward F2 should maintain his position in the center lane as long as possible until the direction of the puck is determined. He should then move laterally following the direction of the puck and attempt to cover or to intercept a clearing pass from the corner. When the puck can be kept in the outside lane on the same side of the rink that the face-off was taken and lost, defenseman D1 should immediately move laterally to the sideboards. He should follow the direction of the puck and attempt to cover or to intercept a clearing pass from the corner. Defenseman D2 should retreat but maintain his defensive position inside the center red line in the center lane.

Note that this formation again resembles a diamond shape that again utilizes only two lanes of the rink—the center lane and the outside lane on the same side of the rink that the face-off was taken and lost.

When the defensive team moves the puck behind the net to the other outside lane, the responsibilities of the two offensive forwards and defensemen must immediately switch. All four players must adjust their positions so that the center lane and the other outside lane are occupied.

As shown in Figure 6.4, offensive forward F2 now has the responsibility of putting pressure on the puck deep in the other outside lane corner. Offensive forward F1 should retreat back to the center lane and maintain his position in the center lane as long as possible until the direction of the puck is determined. He should then move laterally following the direction of the puck and attempt to cover or to intercept a clearing pass from the

Figure 6.4 Losing Face-offs Behind the Offensive Goal

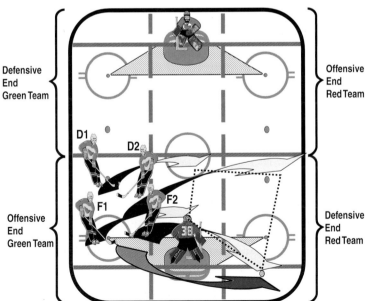

corner. Defenseman D2 should immediately retreat laterally out of the center lane to the sideboards inside the center red line. He should follow the direction of the puck and attempt to cover or to intercept a clearing pass up along the side boards from the corner. Defenseman D1 should retreat slightly and maintain a defensive position inside the center red line in the center lane.

Note that this formation again resembles a diamond shape and again only two lanes of the rink are utilized—the center lane and the outside lane on the other side of the rink that the face-off was taken and lost.

One offensive forward should always be putting pressure on the puck. The other forward should be covering the center lane.

One defenseman should always be at the sideboards on the same side of the rink as the puck and furthest back towards the center red line. The other defenseman should maintain a defensive position in the center lane inside the red line. He will be able to protect the center slot area in the event that the defensive team advances the puck out of their end zone.

Whenever you lose control of the puck you must think defensively even in the other team's end zone.

Remember—the defenseman on the strong side of the rink (the same side of the rink where the puck is) is your safety valve and should always be the furthest back nearest to the center red line.

Face-Offs in the Defensive End

A team on defense in their defensive end must make every attempt to move the puck away from the middle lane slot area in order to prevent a high percentage shot on their goal. Lining up correctly is the first and most important step.

An appropriate lineup is shown in Figure 6.5. In this formation defensive forward F1 will take the face-off. Defenseman D1 will be positioned behind forward F1 towards the center lane just outside the face-off circle. Defenseman D2 will be positioned at the edge of the face-off circle in the slot area directly in front of the net. He should be lined up against the offensive forward opponent in front of the net. Forward F2 should always be positioned next to defenseman D2 on the inside center lane never along the boards. This will allow him to cover the slot and center lane areas and any opponent in this area.

It is important that the goaltender has a clear and unobstructed view of the puck as the face-off is taken. Each defensive player should turn around before the face-off is initiated to ensure that they are not in his line of sight.

Figure 6.5 Face-off Formation in the Defensive End

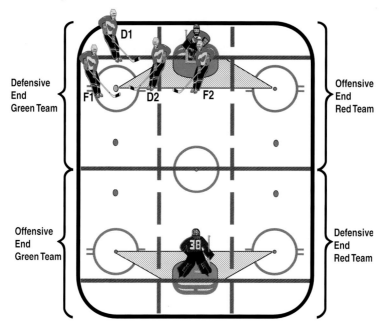

When the Face-Off Is Won in the Defensive End

When the face-off is won, as shown in Figure 6.6, defensive forward F1 will draw the puck back **[P1]** to defenseman D1 and then impede his face-off opponent's progress forward to the puck. Defenseman D1 can now quickly take the puck behind the net or make an immediate clearing pass **[P2]** up this outside lane. As soon as defenseman D1 has control of the puck, forward F1 should move to the near side boards looking for this clearing or breakout pass from defenseman D1. Defenseman D2 should impede any opponent's progress toward the puck while maintaining his defensive position in the center lane slot area. Forward F2 should momentarily impede any opposite opponent and maintain his position in the center lane until the direction of the puck is determined.

Figure 6.6 Winning Face-offs in the Defensive End

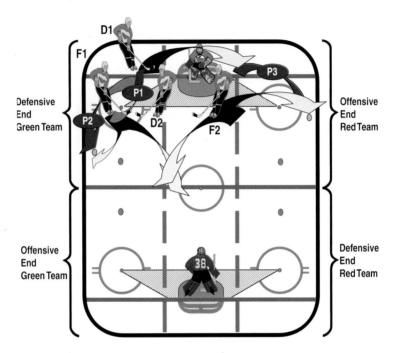

When the puck can be immediately cleared to forward F1 along the side boards, forward F2 should advance up the rink in the center lane looking for a pass from forward F1. When the puck must be moved behind the net, forward F2 should go immediately to the opposite side boards and position himself for a clearing or breakout pass **[P3]** from defenseman D1. When the puck must be moved behind the net, forward F1 should advance up the rink in the center lane looking for a pass from forward F2.

When the Face-Off Is Lost in the Defensive End

When the face-off is lost, each defensive player is still well positioned to check and regain control of the puck. Each defensive player should attempt to force the puck to the outside lanes away from the center lane area, especially the slot area directly in front of the net.

As shown in Figure 6.7, defensive forward F1 should quickly rush forward to put pressure on the opponent defenseman on

the face-off circle side of the rink. If this defenseman has possession of the puck he should force him and the puck to the nearest
outside lane away from the slot area in front of the net. Offensive
forward F2 should also rush forward to protect the top of the
slot area. He will be responsible to check the opponent
defenseman on the other side of the rink. Whenever the puck is
brought near or into the center lane area puck he should force
him and the puck to the outside lane away from the slot area in
front of the net. Defenseman D1 should immediately move to
one side of the slot area directly in front of the net. Defenseman
D2 should maintain his defensive position on the other side of
the slot area in the center lane.

Figure 6.7 Losing Face-offs in the Defensive End

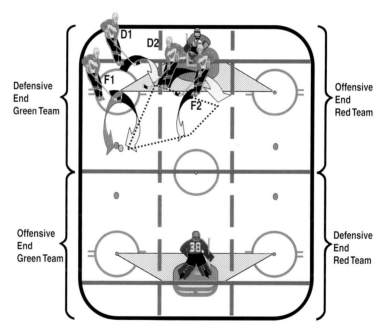

Note that optimum player positioning will resemble a dia-
mond shape formation constructed to protect the slot area.
Each defensive player must protect his portion of the center
lane and the slot area. If the offensive team has possession of the
puck in one of the outside lanes, put pressure on the puck carrier, try to intercept a pass in your area, and try to block any shot

released from your area. Let the offensive team make a mistake with the puck, don't chase it. The protection of your area is your first and most important responsibility.

One defensive player should always be putting pressure on the puck but should not stray from his assigned territory unless the puck is loose and control of it can be regained.

Under no circumstances should a defensive player attempt to skate with the puck or pass the puck into the middle lane inside his own defensive end in order to clear the defensive end.

7

Team Skills III

Killing Penalties

*T*he objective in killing penalties is to play the percentages and stop the other team from scoring. To do this the penalty killers must play as a unit with a single focused strategy.

Penalty killing units are normally composed of 1 or 2 defensemen and 1 forward. The forward must be the point man or chaser putting pressure on the puck in all areas of the rink. This usually requires that this player be one of the best skaters and stick checkers on the defensive team. Every penalty killer must be a good puck handler and not prone to making mistakes with the puck. Every penalty killer must possess a high degree of patience to be good defenders especially in their own end.

There are 3 fundamentals for good penalty killing:

I. Control the Slot Area

One way to do this is to position a defense player in the slot to control that area. This player must stand his ground and prevent any attackers from screening the goaltender, deflecting a puck into the net, receiving a pass in the slot, or getting a rebound.

Another way to do this is to position the penalty killers in a triangle formation around the perimeter of the slot area as shown in Figure 7.1.

The triangle defensive formation is intended to give the attacking team no other option but to carry the puck around the outside of this defensive configuration—to not allow penetration into the slot area for a high percentage scoring opportunity.

In the triangle formation, two penalty killers play low in the triangle to cover the deep attackers while one penalty killer plays high to cover the attacking team's defense or point men. As shown in Figure 7.1, Green Team Defensemen D1 and D2 play low in the triangle while Green Team Forward F1 plays high.

The penalty killer player nearest the puck should challenge the puck carrier to try to force him to make a pass. When the attacking team is forced to make a pass, the penalty killers will have created an opportunity to intercept. The penalty killers should allow the attacking team to pass the puck around the perimeter of the slot area but not into the slot area, always forcing the play to the outside.

Figure 7.1 The Triangle Penalty Defense Formation

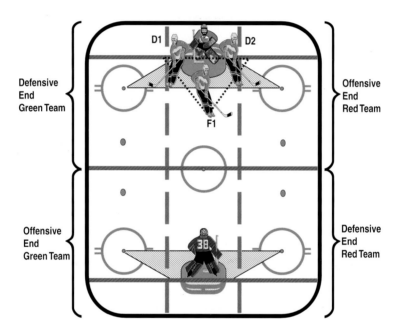

Penalty killers should always keep their bodies between the attacker with the puck and the net. Penalty killers should not focus directly on the puck but instead keep their eyes on the attacker's chest with the puck in their peripheral vision. Penalty killers should always keep their sticks coiled ready to poke check whenever possible.

2. Involve the Goaltender

Involving the goaltender helps to neutralize some of the attacking team's manpower advantage. The penalty killers need to position themselves to give the goaltender a clear view of the puck so that he will have a reasonable chance of stopping all shots.

Once a shot has been taken the penalty killers must cover and clear all rebounds. As shown in Figure 7.2, a rebound must be shot quickly to a safe area.

Figure 7.2 Clearing the Offensive Rebound

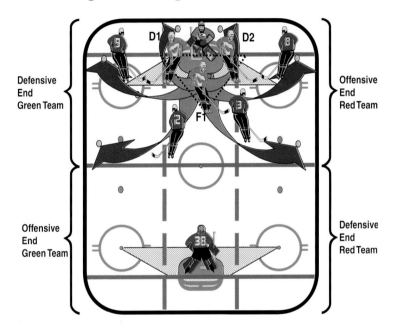

Safe areas include behind the net, to a corner, or to an outside lane.

The puck should never be cleared or shot through the slot area or the middle lane anywhere near the front of the net. The penalty killers should not attempt to gain control of the puck in the slot or to skate out of danger with it. They must first clear it to one of the safe areas and only then attempt to gain control of it.

Once control of the puck has been gained it must be cleared out of the defensive end and shot as far down the rink as possible.

Clear communication between the penalty killers and the goaltender is essential to make sure that there will be no loose pucks in front of the net. The goaltender should freeze all pucks that he can, the penalty killers should prevent any members of the attacking team from impeding his efforts or knocking any pucks loose or out of his catching glove.

3.Take Time Off the Clock

The penalty killers should attempt to deny the attacking team a high percentage shot on net. This will force the attacking team to maneuver for a better scoring opportunity. This will take precious seconds off the clock.

The penalty killers should also try to get as many face-offs as possible. Each face-off will take 5 to 10 seconds off the clock.

The best strategy is to simply clear the puck out of the defensive end at every opportunity and then pressure the attacking team in their end. Every time the puck is cleared, it will tire out the attacking team who will have to skate back into their defensive end to retrieve the puck. More importantly every time the puck is cleared, it will take 10 to 20 seconds off the clock.

8

Player Skills I

Checking an Opponent

*C*hecking an opponent is a skill that must be learned and practiced. It does not come naturally. The length of a hockey player's career, even at the highest professional levels, is usually determined by that player's ability to execute consistent and effective defense. Offense alone is not enough. Two-way players are rewarded with more playing time by most coaches.

At an individual level defense mostly depends upon effort, tenacity, and skating ability. Defensive players must be willing to energetically skate the entire rink surface to deter their opponents. Defensive players must backcheck—skate back into their defensive end zone to check an offensive opponent player.

The first element of individual defense is positioning. Defenders should always attempt to stay "inside" their opponents on the rink surface at all times. This means that your opponents will always be between you and the boards. This forces your opponents to occupy one of the outside lanes near the boards and inhibits your opponent's ability to skate into the center lane and the slot area.

Defenders should also always attempt to occupy a position between their opponent and the defensive team's goal. As shown in Figure 8.1, the defensive Red Team has done both of these things well. Each Red Team player has taken a defensive position "inside" his Green Team opponent and between his Green Team opponent and the Red Team goalie. As a result the Green Team can only occupy the outside lanes and will have difficulty getting the puck to the slot area. This positioning provides the Red Team players an opportunity to impede a shot on goal or a pass or perhaps to stop the shot or pass altogether. Because these outside lanes have proven to provide only low percentage scoring opportunities, any shot that does make it through will also have a low chance of scoring a goal.

In order to gain good defensive positioning the Red Team players have had to skate back from their offensive end with much effort and tenacity. They did not abandon the puck once they lost possession of it in their offensive end. They had to skate faster and further to catch up with their opponents and to gain this "inside" position. This "inside" position now makes them obstacles that the offensive Green Team players must now go around as they try to bring the puck to the slot area for a high percentage shot on the Red Team goal.

Figure 8.1 The Inside Defensive Position

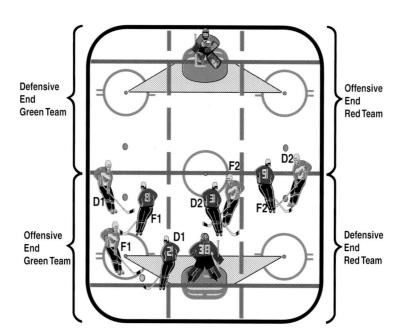

The second element of effective individual defense is to move at an angle in the same direction as the opponent puck carrier forcing him to an outside lane. What you should try to do is to get the opponent puck carrier to skate directly into you rather than trying to skate into the puck carrier yourself. Make your opponent come to you. When you skate directly at an opponent puck carrier in an attempt to check him, you will restrict the amount of time you will have available to effect a checking action. This gives the advantage to the puck carrier who now can step aside quickly to let you go by before you can react and change your own skating direction. The less time you have to effect a check the harder it will be to execute.

Sometimes the opponent puck carrier might be unable to avoid the defender coming straight at him at the last instant. In these cases you may see spectacular collisions of these two players. Although the check has been made this is not an effective checking tactic. More often than not it is accidental—a result of great luck or misfortune depending upon whether you are the defender or the attacking player. It is a much better tactic to skate in the same direction as the attacking player while forcing him to one of the outside lanes as you attempt to check him off the puck—let him come to you.

Skating Backward to Check an Opponent

For defensemen skating backward is a natural occurrence much of the time. As defensemen attempt to check an opponent, they will usually turn and skate backwards allowing the opponent puck carrier to come forward towards him.

As shown in Figure 8.2, the Red Team defenseman is skating backwards in the same direction as the Green Team opponent with the puck. He has taken an "inside" position keeping the Green Team opponent between himself and the boards and is allowing the puck carrier to advance towards him. He has also positioned himself between the Green Team opponent and his own goalkeeper.

Figure 8.2 Skating Backward to Check an Opponent

Skating
Backward
at an angle in
the Same
Direction to
Make a Check

If the Red Team defenseman can skate back at the same speed or just slightly slower than the Green Team attacker is skating he will allow the gap between them to close slowly. This will maximize the length of time he is in close proximity to the Green Team attacker and will enhance his opportunity to effect the check.

Skating Forward to Check an Opponent

Forwards must usually stop their skating direction when they lose possession of the puck to an opponent then turn in order to skate forward in the same direction as the opponent puck carrier.

As shown in Figure 8.3, the Red Team forward is skating forward in the same direction as his Green Team opponent with the puck. He has taken an "inside" position keeping the Green Team opponent between himself and the boards and is attempting to direct the puck carrier to the boards and away from his own goal-keeper. He has also positioned himself between the Green Team opponent and his own goalkeeper.

Figure 8.3 Skating Forward to Check an Opponent

Skating
Forward
at an angle in
the Same
Direction to
Make a Check

If the Red Team forward can skate forward at the same speed or just slightly faster than the Green Team attacker is skating he will allow the gap between them to close slowly. This will maximize the length of time he is in close proximity to the Green Team attacker and will enhance his opportunity to effect the check.

The Magic Checking Triangle

Individual defensive skills are also augmented by stick dexterity. Stick checking is an attempt to gain control of the puck by first making the opponent lose control of it. There are two basic types of stick checks: sweep check and poke check. To be effective both rely upon the defensive player's ability to position his stick in an area under his opponent's stick in front of his body. This area is shown in red in Figure 8.4 and can be referred to as the "magic triangle".

Figure 8.4 The Magic Checking Triangle

The Magic
Triange

When the defensive player can position his stick in this "magic triangle" he can easily lift his opponents stick to make him lose control of the puck. He can then sweep the puck to one side with a sweeping action or poke the puck back behind the offensive player with a quick pushing action.

Remember to first gain a good defensive position "inside" your opponent and between your opponent and your goal. Put your opponent between you and the boards.

Always attempt to skate at an angle in the same direction as your opponent before you attempt to make a check. Make your opponent skate directly into you. Coming straight at him at high speed will drastically reduce the time you will have to make a check.

Check your opponent off the puck using a sweep or poke check after you have placed your stick in the "magic triangle".

9
Player Skills II

Playmaking

Good players usually control the pace and flow of the game because they control the movement of the puck up and down the rink surface. They do this by getting and maintaining possession of the puck more often than other players. They also do this by passing the puck at the appropriate time to a teammate who can further the advance of the puck into their opponents end zone or who can immediately make a high percentage shot on net. Passing the puck forward to a teammate who is closer to your opponent's goal is called "head-manning" the puck. Players who create or initiate the plays that result in goals being scored are known to have good *"playmaking"* skills. Effective playmaking skills rely on several key abilities.

Stickhandling

Good players move the puck small distances with a skill called *"stickhandling"*. This involves the transfer of the puck from one side of the stick blade to the other by moving the wrists from side to side. The puck can be quickly moved in all directions using this skill—from side to side as well as from front to back or any combination of these four directions. This rapid movement of the puck allows the puck carrier to maintain possession of the puck and avoid being checked by an opponent.

Stickhandling is not a skill that comes naturally to everyone.

Good stickhandlers have supple wrists that allow them to move the puck softly from the forehand to the backhand easily under control while they skate. This is a trait that is not naturally acquired and must be learned through practice.

The proper type of hockey stick is required to maximize stickhandling skills. Stick length is an important factor. Many players utilize a stick that is much too long. Great stickhandlers will play with a shorter stick that will barely reach their chin when standing on their skates. Most good stickhandlers also find that playing with a stick having an oversized blade will improve their ability to control the puck. The blade must be taped on the entire blade so that maximum friction can be maintained between the puck and the stick. Great stickhandlers also find that playing with a stick having a straight or minimum curved blade will improve their stickhandling skills. A stick having a blade that is curved to the maximum allowed might aid the slapshot but it will severely inhibit control of the puck especially on the backhand side of the stick.

A shorter stick with a straighter blade is best.

Great playmakers know when to stickhandle. If there are no opposition players in the vicinity, get used to simply pushing the puck in front of you while skating forward. Don't waste energy by stickhandling if it is not necessary.

Peripheral Vision and Rink Awareness

Good playmakers also have excellent peripheral vision and rink awareness. This allows them to see all their teammates and their opposition players on the rink and in addition to know where they are headed. They are able to assess the flow of the play with a single look and are able to see where they can pass or skate to avoid being checked. The basis of this is to be able to keep your head up while you are handling the puck. Skating with your head down as you carry the puck is a certain turnover.

Using a Bank Pass

Good playmakers also utilize other objects to "bank" or careen the puck off in order to move or pass the puck to a teammate who can further the advance of the puck into their opponent's end zone or who can immediately make a high percentage shot on net. These other objects can include opposition player's legs and skates, the back of the goal net, or the boards. As shown in Figure 9.1, the Green Team defenseman D1 with the puck has made a bank pass [P1] using the boards and then skated around and past his opponent Red Team forward F1 to retrieve the puck.

Use the proper angle, bank the puck off the object, and then skate quickly to retrieve it. The boards are never too far away and they always give a return pass. A simple bank pass back to you or to a teammate can create an opening for a scoring opportunity.

Remember, the boards are your best friends.

Figure 9.1 The Bank Pass off the Boards

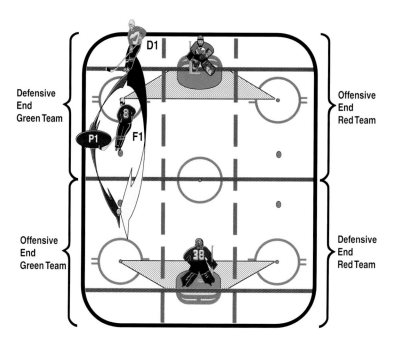

Skating Speed

Skating speed is also an important factor. Most players when approached by an opposition player will slow down in an attempt to gain improved puck control. Great playmakers will do just the opposite and speed up to go around or through an opposition player. They will veer to one side holding the puck as far away from the opposition player as possible keeping their own body between the puck and this player. Once they are even with the opposition player they will speed up using a jump crossover step that will quickly bring them forward and behind the opposition player. The element of increased speed combined with a cut or veer in behind the opposition player again positions their own body between the puck and the opposition player and aids their ability to maintain control or protect their possession of the puck.

Speed up to go around and step in behind your opponent once you are past him.

10
Player Skills III

Scoring Goals

*I*n its simplest form, scoring is putting the puck behind the goal tender into the goal. The ability to score goals is a rare skill appreciated by players, coaches, and fans alike. Some players seem to be born with the knack of putting the puck into the net. Most players must practice this skill at every opportunity to be an effective goal scorer.

It is very common that the best or most prolific scorers are not blessed with the hardest shots. Possessing a reasonably hard shot will help you to be a goal scorer but you must also be able to release your shot quickly.

Scoring will depend upon three factors:

1. the accuracy and aim of the shot,

2. the timing or quickness of the release of the shot, and

3. the spot or position on the rink surface from which the shot is taken.

If done correctly, the puck will arrive with accuracy at a scoring spot in front of the goal that the goalie isn't currently covering and that the goalie can't get to before the puck crosses the goal line.

The Five Shooting Holes

The highest opportunity targets are spots between the pipes and under the crossbar that the goalie must move to in order to cover or block when your shot is released. These are the places that the goalie doesn't already occupy at the moment that your shot is released. These are also the places that require the goalie to move the greatest distance to get to when your shot is released. The best scoring targets are called shooting holes and are usually numbered in a clock-wise direction 1 through 5 as shown in Figure 10.1.

As you face the goalie, shooting hole #1 is on the low left side. Shooting hole #2 is on the high left side. Shooting hole #3 is on the high right side. Shooting hole #4 is on the low right side. Shooting hole #5 is between the goalie's legs.

Figure 10.1 The Five Shooting Holes

As a general rule shooting holes #1 and #4 will usually require the goalie to move the greatest lateral or sideways distance. A second rule is that shooting holes on the stick side of the goalie are usually the most difficult for the goalie to cover.

This means that for a right handed goalie who catches with his left hand as shown in Figure 10.1, shooting holes #1 and #2 will be on his stick side and will present the best scoring opportunities. For a left handed goalie who catches with his right hand, shooting holes #3 and #4 will be on his stick side and will present the best scoring opportunities. Shooting hole #5 presents a very special opportunity for the shooter that will be discussed in the next section of this handbook.

No matter how hard you shoot the puck, if you miss the net you can never score.

No matter how hard you shoot the puck, if you hit the goalie directly with the puck it is very unlikely that you will score.

To get the best chance to score a goal, you must make the goalie move to stop your shot.

Goaltender Net Minding Styles

Your choice of the best shooting hole at which to aim your shot will vary with each goalie you will face. This is because each goalie will present a different goalie stature or size and each goalie will utilize a different over-all net minding style. Goalies can be tall or short in stature. Goalies will also generally and consistently present a butterfly or stand-up net minding style. As a general rule tall goalies will have a stand-up net minding style. Stand-up goalies tend to stay on their feet as much as possible and rely on their bulk and hand quickness to catch or block most shots. As a result tall stand-up goalies will usually cover the high shooting holes with a minimum of movement. A tall right handed stand-up goalie will usually cover the #3 hole nearest his glove with little difficulty. He will usually also be able to cover shooting hole #2 nearest his blocker with a minimum of movement.

A tall stand-up goalie will usually not be most adept at moving side-to-side. As a result he will probably have the most difficulty covering the low shooting holes #1 and #4 that are furthest from his glove and blocker.

As a general rule shorter goalies will usually present a butterfly net minding style. Butterfly goalies tend to flop down spreading their pads (like the wings of a butterfly) as much as possible and will rely upon their leg and hand quickness to catch or block most shots. As a result shorter butterfly goalies will usually cover the low shooting holes with a minimum of movement. A short right handed butterfly goalie will usually cover the #4 hole nearest his left pad and glove with little difficulty. He will usually also be able to cover shooting hole #1 nearest his right pad and blocker with a minimum of movement.

Shorter butterfly goalies will probably have the most difficulty covering the high shooting holes #2 and #3 that will be furthest from their glove and blocker especially after they have flopped down.

Shooting hole #5 is the area between the goalie's leg pads. This shooting hole is the hardest target to hit accurately because this area will move and change size as the goalie moves. As a result this choice of shooting target should only be considered under very special circumstances.

The key to maximize the effective use of shooting hole #5 is to get the goalie to move before you release your shot. The best way to get a goalie to move is to fake a shot to one side of the net and shoot to the other. Generally this will be a fake to the shooter's backhand and a sweep of the puck back to the forehand side prior to the release of the shot.

A stand-up goalie will push off one skate to move side-to-side. This push will maximize the area between his leg pads and will also move this shooting hole in the direction the goalie has pushed. If you release your shot with great accuracy at this shooting hole at the exact moment the goalie begins to move side-to-side; you will maximize your chances of scoring. Right-handed people have learned to push off their right foot to throw or catch a ball. As a result most right-handed goalies also tend to like to push to their left off their right skate. If you can get them to push to their right off their left skate you will also increase your chances of scoring. The opposite is true for left-handed goalies. If you can get them to push to their left off their right skate you will also increase your chances of scoring.

A butterfly goalie will sometimes lift his goal stick just before he begins to flop down to cover the front of the net. It seems a natural movement for all of us to lift up just before we go down. If you release your shot along the surface of the rink with great accuracy at this shooting hole at the exact moment the goalie begins to lift up, you will also increase your chances of scoring.

Combinations of these statures and net minding styles make your choice of best shooting hole even more difficult. A tall goalie may utilize a butterfly net minding style. A shorter goalie may utilize a stand-up net minding style. Both short and tall goalies with either stand-up or butterfly styles that have been blessed with especially quick hands and feet are very difficult to score upon.

Prior to every game the most prolific goal scorers will carefully watch the opposition goalie during his pre-game warm-up to try to determine his basic net minding style and his level of hand and foot quickness. Once these have been determined, the shooting holes that will present the best scoring opportunities during the game will become evident.

The best scoring strategy is to find a way to make the goalie move first before you release your shot and then to aim at the shooting hole that presents the greatest scoring opportunity. For example, if you can get a tall right-handed stand-up goalie to move to cover shooting hole #1 before you release your shot, then your best scoring opportunity will be shooting hole #4. Conversely if you can get him to move to cover shooting hole #4 before you release your shot, then shooting hole #1 will offer your best scoring opportunity. If you cannot get him to move at all, then shooting hole #1 will usually present your greatest scoring opportunity.

The best rule to follow if you are unsure where to shoot is to aim at shooting hole #1 on a right handed goalie and shooting hole #4 on a left handed goalie.

Remember stick side low is usually every goalie's greatest weakness!

Shooting Locations

As important as it is to know where to aim your shot and when to release your shot, is to know from where to shoot.

Figure 10.2 The Best Shooting Locations

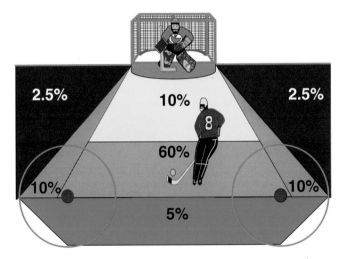

As shown in Figure 10.2, more goals are scored in the ● slot area from 10 to 15 feet out in front of the net than from all other areas on the rink surface combined. This area in the slot area accounts for about 60% of all goals scored in hockey. The remaining ● of the slot area up to 10 feet out in front of the net will account for another 10% of all goals scored. When shots are released outside the slot area these percentages are drastically reduced.

The ● area near each face-off circle will account for approximately 20% (10% on each side) while the ● area between the goal line and the face-off circles will account for approximately

5% (2.5% on each side). The ● area 15 to 25 feet further out in front of the net from the top of the slot area to the leading or top edges of the face-off circles will account for the remaining 5% of all goals scored.

The ideal distance from which to shoot will change depending on the goalie's positioning in front of the net, the goalie's skill level, the shooter's skill level and the speed of his shot.

The three major reasons why most scoring opportunities are missed are as follows:

1. Many players have the habit of moving in too close to the net before they shoot (as if in an attempt to stickhandle past the goaltender). They make the mistake of moving to within 10 feet of the net believing that they have to be as close to the net as possible in order to score. Moving to within 10 feet of the net automatically increases the goaltender's coverage of the net area because it restricts or narrows the *"shooter's angle"* or available path the puck will have to one of the open net areas.

2. Many players have the habit of waiting too long before they release their shot on goal. The shooter's angle is automatically narrowed when the goaltender moves out towards the shooter. Waiting to release the shot will give the goaltender time to move out towards the shooter to cut down his angle.

3. Many players have the habit of always attempting to get the puck on their forehand or strong side of their stick before they release their shot on goal. They do this to get their hardest possible shot on goal. Taking the time to do this can take you out of the highest percentage scoring slot area and into a low-percentage scoring area on one side of the net. It also increases the time an opponent will have to make a check.

To maximize a scoring chance, get into a high percentage scoring location before you shoot. Shots taken from a distance greater than 25 feet have little chance of making it past any goaltender having average abilities. More importantly the majority of shots taken from less than 10 feet out are usually stopped by most goaltenders unless they come during a goalmouth scramble on a rebound shot. Shots taken from either side of the net will always have a lower probability of scoring.

If you can see a teammate in a higher percentage location than you, pass the puck to him and follow your pass in for a possible rebound. If you cannot see a teammate in a better position, and cannot get yourself into a high percentage area, shoot low stick side at the goaltender's pads and follow your shot for a possible rebound.

Remember to have the best chance to score you must shoot from the highest percentage location that you can. Most goals are scored from shots released directly in front of the net.

Don't try to stickhandle past the goalie—always try to shoot from 10 to 15 feet out in front of the net in the slot area.

If the goalie comes out towards you to challenge the shot, release your shot immediately—waiting longer will only give him the advantage.

Choosing the Type of Shot

The type of shot you select to use during a scoring opportunity will depend upon where the goalie is when you are about to release your shot and how far away you are from the net. You choice of shot can also help you to create an element of surprise which will increase your scoring chances.

Possible shot choices include the wrist, flip, snap, slap, and backhand shot.

The wrist shot is the most accurate shot. It is the preferred shot to use from the slot area where accuracy is most important and where there is usually little time to release a shot. Because it does not require a back swing or wind-up it can also help to create an element of surprise that will impede the goaltender's defensive actions.

Further away from the slot the slap shot can be more effective. Given enough time to wind up with a big back swing, the slap shot will propel the puck toward the net faster than any other shot. As a general rule, there will never be enough time to take a slap shot between the top of the face-off circles and the goal line. The slap shot is most effective from long range when used as a shot intended to create a rebound for teammates breaking to the goal.

If there is not enough time for a big wind-up, the snap shot can be used. It reduces the time required to execute and still produces more puck speed than a wrist shot.

The flip shot is an essential shot to master if you plan to deke the goaltender within 10 feet of the net. This shot will enable you to easily flip the puck over an outstretched glove, blocker, or leg pad near the crease area. This shot will also allow you to score from a rebound once the goalie has flopped down.

The backhand shot and the backhand flip are a good shot to use when you are in close to the net. Most goaltenders are not used to seeing backhand shots regularly in practices or games. As a result most goaltenders have difficulty in determining the exact moment of release and the shot target with a backhand shot. Backhand shots will almost always surprise a goaltender. Unfortunately this is a very hard shot to master and must be practiced with passion.

One thing most goal scorers have in common is their ability to disguise from the goaltender when they are about to release their shot. Quick release of any shot will regularly catch the goalie off-guard.

The one-time shot is the preferred quick release shot when the puck is passed from behind the net or across the slot to the shooter. This shot requires that the pass is received and the shot is released all in one flowing motion by the shooter. The goaltender will have to face the shooter in action and will have little time to prepare for the shot.

Another effective way to catch the goaltender off-guard is to shoot in stride. Shooting in stride or off one foot is a good way to reduce the time the goaltender will have to prepare for the shot. This shot requires the shooter to release the shot without changing the rhythm of his skating motion with his weight on or over his foot nearest the puck. This will usually catch the goaltender off-guard, as he will be expecting the shooter to continue to carry the puck.

Goaltenders are beaten because of the human limits to reaction time.

A well placed shot, released from a high percentage area, with adequate speed is almost impossible to stop.

11

Player Skills IV

Goaltending

Goaltending is the skill of stopping the puck from crossing the goal line. Goaltenders must block, cover, or catch the puck before the puck enters the net behind them. Many goaltenders rely upon their natural quickness and agility to react to the shot as it is released on the net. Great goaltenders will also anticipate the release of the shot and position themselves so that the puck can either only hit them or miss the net completely. This is known as cutting down the shooter's angle so that he has no open net at which to aim his shot.

As the goaltender retreats back towards his net, the coverage area decreases significantly. As the coverage area diminishes, the scoring opportunity becomes greater. With a diminished coverage area, the shooter can "see" more open portions of the net at which to aim his shot.

As shown in Figure 11.1, the shooter is in front of the net at the top of the slot about 15 feet from the goal line. The goal-

Figure 11.1 Goaltender With 100% Coverage of the Net

100% Coverage
With Goaltender
12 Feet Out

tender would have to stand about 12 feet out directly in front of the shooter to cover the entire net. More importantly the distance between the goaltender and the shooter will be 3 feet or less.

As shown in Figure 11.2, at 6 feet out in front of the net, the goaltender can cover little more than 50% of the net. The shooter will have almost half of the net as open at which to aim his shot. More importantly the distance between shooter and goaltender will be less than 10 feet.

Figure 11.2 Goaltender With 50% Coverage of the Net

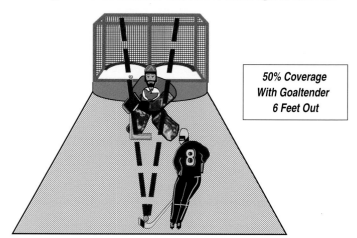

50% Coverage
With Goaltender
6 Feet Out

As shown in Figure 11.2, at approximately 1 or 2 feet out the goaltender will be able to cover only about 10% of the open net. It is important to note that in this case the distance between shooter and goaltender will be more than 10 feet and less than 15 feet.

In similar fashion, with the goaltender on or slightly in front of the goal line, the coverage area increases significantly as the shooter advances towards the goal.

As shown in Figure 11.3, the shooter released his shot from in front of the net at the top of the slot about 15 feet from the goal line while the goaltender remained at 1 or 2 feet out in front of the net. In this case the goaltender can only cover approximately 10% of the net area.

Figure 11.3 Goaltender With 10% Coverage of the Net

10% Coverage
With Goaltender
1 Foot Out

As shown in Figure 11.4, when the shooter advances with the puck and releases his shot within 10 feet of the goal line, the goaltender at 1 or 2 feet out in front of the net can now cover approximately 50% of the net area.

Figure 11.4 Shooter With 50% Scoring Opportunity

50% Coverage
With Shooter
Within 10 Feet

When the shooter advances with the puck and releases his shot within 5 feet of the net he will have very little chance of scoring. As shown in Figure 11.5, the goaltender at 1 or 2 feet out in front of the net will now be able to cover approximately 100% of the net area.

Figure 11.5 Shooter With 0% Scoring Opportunity

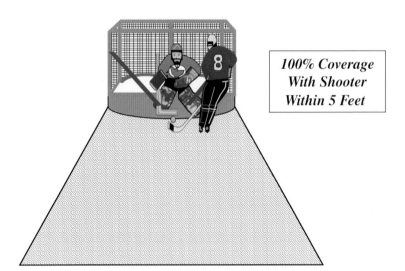

100% Coverage With Shooter Within 5 Feet

In both cases the goaltender did not have to advance towards the shooter. The shooter automatically improved the goaltender's coverage of the net area dramatically simply by advancing toward the net and waiting to release his shot.

It is the relative distance between shooter and goaltender that determines coverage area.

In order to cover the maximum net area the goaltender must use a "telescoping" technique. The goaltender must attempt to adjust the relative distance between the shooter and himself at the moment the shot is released without advancing too far out in front of the net. Too close in and the goaltender will give up too much net area for a long-range shot. Too far out and the goaltender may give the shooter too much rink area to skate around him and put the puck into the net. This is called "giving up the back door."

The goaltender must continually adjust his position as the play develops so that he is positioned at the optimum distance from the shooter. Great goaltenders will purposefully stay back in the net to invite a shot from longer out then anticipate the release of the shot and quickly move out toward the shooter to cut down the shooter's angle to the net.

Cut down the shooter's angle to the net by moving toward the shooter to at the moment the shot is released.

The set position of the goaltender's body or his basic stance will also enhance his ability to consistently stop pucks from crossing the goal line. Feet should be shoulder-width apart with toes pointed out slightly. Knees and waist should be slightly flexed to promote good balance. This forces weight to be placed on the balls of the feet. The blocker should be held to the side slightly in front of the knee. The catcher should also be held to the side and slightly in front of the knee.

The position of the goaltender's stick is also as important as the position of the goaltender's body. The stick is the primary tool used to defend the net: deflecting shots, clearing the puck to an open teammate, and poke checking an onrushing attacker who has come too close.

The stick should be held firmly at the top of the shank or paddle (the wider part) with the second finger on the wider part. In the ready position the stick should be flat on the floor with neither the toe nor the heel up off the rink surface. The stick blade should be about 12 to 13 inches in front of the goaltender's skates and slanted slightly backward. Slanting the stick helps to deflect shots up and over the net rather than letting them bounce back for a rebound. However, when the puck is rolling slowly forward, the stick should be kept vertical. This prevents a slow rolling puck from rolling up and over the goaltender into the net.

Keep body and stick square to every potential shooter.

Appendix A

Coaches Corner:

Player Quicktips

Player Quicktips
Offense

- Always Try To Advance The Puck Forward Into Your Opponent's End—Pass Ahead To A Teammate

- When In Doubt, Shoot First, Think Later—Take The Shot Even If It's Not A Good One—Follow Your Shot To The Net And Stop In Front For The Rebound

- 2nd Forward In Should Charge The Net For The Rebound

- If You Have A Teammate With You On A Scoring Opportunity, Shoot Early So That One Or Both Of You Are Still In Front Of The Net For The Rebound

- Never Chase The Puck Into The Corner In Your Own End, Let Your Defense Go Get It

- Don't Chase The Puck Behind The Opponents Net If Your Teammate Is Already There

- Forecheck, Don't Give The Opponents Time To Get Organized

- Don't Cherry Pick—Skate Back Into Your Defensive End When You Lose possession Of The Puck—Your Defense Needs Your Help To Break Out Of Your End

- Backcheck, Help The Defense Out, Cover The Opponent's Forwards 1st, Then The Opponents Defensemen

- Only One Man After The Puck At Any Time, Everyone Else Should Find An Opponent To Cover In Our End Or An Open Space To Receive A Pass In The Opponent's End

- Stay Spread Out. Occupy At Least Two Adjacent Lanes. Don't Get Bunched Up!

- Pass Back To Your Defensemen, Especially In The Opponent's End

- **Always Keep Moving; (Skate In Circles If Necessary)**
- **Communicate With Your Teammates!**

Player Quicktips Defense

- Never Pass Across The Slot (The Middle) In Your Own Defensive End—Keep The Puck Along The Boards

- Don't Screen Your Goalie (Block Your Goalie's View To The Puck) In Your Own Defensive End Unless You Plan To Block The Shot Yourself—Let Him See The Puck At All Times

- Only One Defenseman After The Puck In The Corner In Your Own Defensive End At Any Time, The Other defenseman Should Go To The Front Of Our Net And Look For An Opponent To Cover Or A Loose Puck To Clear

- Hold The Point Inside The Opponents End (Inside The Red Line); Give Your Forwards Someone To Pass To

- Take The Shot From The Point, Don't Try To stickhandle All The Way To The Opponent's Goal—Give Your Forwards A Chance For A Rebound

- Always Keep Moving; (Don't Get Caught Flat-Footed)

- Don't Panic Around Your Own Net—Shoot The Puck Out Of The Slot First –Then Get Control Of The Puck And Break Out

- When In Doubt Clear The Puck In Your Own Defensive End– Don't Get Fancy—Even If You Have To Shoot It All The Way Down The Rink

- Stay Slightly Ahead Or Slightly Behind The Other Defenseman. Always Keep The Option Open To Make A Lateral Pass between You If One Of You Cannot Advance The Puck Or Take A Shot On Net

- Communicate With Your Teammates!

Player Quicktips
Goaltender

- Freeze The Puck In Your Crease—Don't Try Anything Fancy
- Freeze The Puck When Your Team Needs A Stoppage Or Help To Get Organized
- Always Keep The Middle Of Your Chest In Line With The Puck
- Always Keep Your Eye On The Puck
- At The Moment You Think The Shot Will Be Released, Move Out Slowly Towards The Shooter. Always Try To Cut Down The Shooter's Angle
- If Your Back Hurts From Bending Over, Stretch When The Puck Is Down The Other End
- Keep Your Stick Down On The Floor At All Times
- Keep Your Glove Hand Out Ready For Anything
- If Your Defense Is Screening You, Yell Their Name Or Number And Tell Them To Move!
- Don't Plant Yourself In Your Skates; Stay On Your Toes
- Don't Make Your Move Until The Guy Coming At You Has Made His
- If They Score On You, Move On. . . . It Won't Happen If You Try Again!
- If Their Offense Gets In Your Goalie Box Don't Be Afraid To Push 'em Out!
- Talk To Your Players, You Are Their Extra Set Of Eyes. Tell Them Where The Puck Is When They Don't Have It Or Can't See It For Themselves.
- Communicate With Your Teammates!

Player Quicktips
Shooting On Goal

- Look Up Directly At Your Target Just Before You Shoot

- Aim At One Of The Five Shooting Holes, Don't Just Let It Rip

- Shooting Accurately Is More Important Than Shooting Hard

- Get Your Shot Away As Quickly As You Can, Don't Wind Up To Shoot . . . This Can Give The Goalie Too Much Time To Get Ready

- Release Your Shot By Pushing Off Your Back Or Inside Foot—The Foot Nearest Your Stick—Bend Your Leg And Step Towards Your Target—If You Shift Your Weight You Will Get More Power

- Don't Scoop The Puck To Get Lift On Your Wrist Shots— Roll Your Hands Backward Or Inward And "Snap" Your Wrists Quickly And Hard To Get Extra Lift

- Wrist Shots Are More Accurate Than Slap Shots—Use Them!

- Backhand Shots Are Harder For The Goalie To Stop— Use Them When They Are Available

- Snap Shots Are Like Slap Shots Without The Windup - These Are Important As You Can Get Your Shot Off Faster And Still Produce A Lot Of Power

- Move Your Lower Hand Down Your Stick For Better Slap Shots

- Most People Get Harder Slap Shots By Improving Their Technique—Strength Is Less Important Than Form

- You Are Supposed To Hit The Floor Slightly When Taking A Slap Shot

Player Quicktips
Shooting Holes

- Shoot Acurately—Aim At The Shooting Holes—Don't Just Blast Away

- Holes #1 & #4 Will Give You The Best Scoring Chance If You Shoot Quickly And Accurately

- Holes #2 & #3 Will Give You The Next Best Scoring Chance But Are Difficult To Hit And Easier For Most Goalies To Stop

- Hole #5 Should Be Your Last Choice But Only If This Hole Is Open And The Goalie Has Already Started To Move

- The Goalie's Belly Button Is Not Hole #6

- Always Try To Make The Goalie Move To Stop Your Shot

Appendix B

Favorite
Practice
Drills

Skate and Brake Drill

I have always found that skating is the one essential skill that makes all the others effective. Players who can stop and turn as well as change direction back to front with confidence will master all the other skills more effectively. In my opinion skating speed, although desirable, is not the most important player skill. At the start and end of each practice I use this signal skate drill to help my players gain the confidence they need on their skates to play the game at their full speed.

This drill requires the players to line up side by side at one end of the rink on the goal line. As shown in Figure B.1 one of the coaches faces the players at the center red line to give them signals which will direct their skating direction. Either the coach's hand or hockey stick can be held high in the air as the signal beacon.

Figure B.1 Skate and Brake Drill

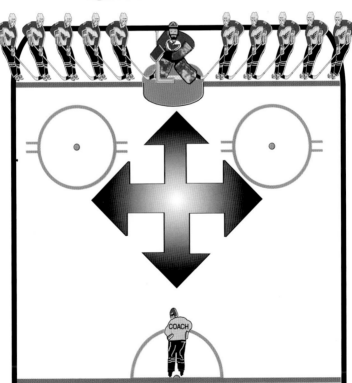

The signals are as follows:

hand or stick pointing up—players skate forward;

hand or stick pointing down—players stop;

hand or stick pointing to the left—players execute crossover step left skate in front of right skate;

hand or stick pointing to the right—players execute crossover step right skate in front of left skate.

As shown in Figure B.1 by the directional arrows, it is important that players skate in continuous straight lines of direction—up and down the rink as well as side to side. Do not let them circle to stop or advance forward on the crossover steps.

When players reach the center red line they automatically reverse their skating direction and skate backwards to the other end of the rink while continuing to follow the coach's signals.

When practicing on a half rink surface, players can automatically reverse their direction without turning around at the center red line and skate backwards to their original end zone goal line while continuing to follow the coach's signals.

Four Corner Drill

The four-corner drill can be utilized to practice and learn stickhandling skills. This drill requires you to set up a box on the rink surface about 12 inches square. I have used pucks, cones,

Figure B.2 Four Corner Drill: Moving the Puck Around the Corners

and tape but have had most success with a 12-inch square piece of ceramic floor tile.

As shown in Figure B.2, the players must stand stationary and close enough to the box to reach all the four corners with the blade of their stick. They must move the puck around the perimeter of the box clockwise and then counterclockwise with each drill repetition.

Players can start slowly glancing at the puck. As they feel more comfortable, encourage them to increase their speed. Remind the players to try to keep their head up during the entire drill using only their peripheral vision to monitor or see the puck.

Tips Down Drill

Stickhandling skills are advanced when a player can keep his head up and see the puck using his peripheral (bottom eye) vision. The easiest way to do this is to teach the players to keep the puck in front of them rather than drag it by their side using their stick blade. If the puck is in front of them they will be able to see it more easily.

Figure B.3 Tips Down Drill: Peripheral Vision Through the Cones

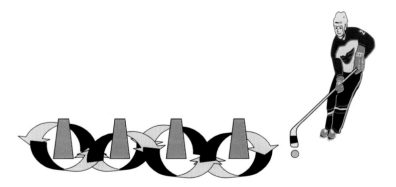

As shown in Figure B.3, in teaching this skill I utilize orange cones placed about 3 feet apart in a straight line stretching from the center red line to the end zone goal line. This drill requires the players to first turn the blade of their sticks over so that the tip or end of the blade is down pointing to the rink surface. Each player then takes a puck through the cones by pressing down his blade tip on the top of the puck with enough pressure to allow it to move. Encourage each player to keep his head up while following the puck skating as quickly as he can through the cones. Repetitions of this drill will give players a feel for the puck at the end of their sticks without having to look at it. It will also encourage players to keep the puck in front of their bodies while skating through the cones.

Once this has been mastered, players can now return the blade of their sticks to its normal position and again follow a puck through the cones skating as fast as they can.

Once players can stickhandle effectively through the cones skating as fast as they can with their sticks in their normal position, have them do this drill with their sticks tip down as before. With this repetition through the cones allow them to stickhandle as they normally would using only the tip of their stick blade to move the puck—do not allow them to touch the top of the puck. Successful completion of multiple drill repetitions will allow them to elevate their stickhandling skills to an even higher level.

Go in Flow Drill

I am always reminding my players to try to establish a flow of play up and down the rink surface. In hockey terms this is known as playing a "north-south" game. I remind them that they must be aware of the position of their teammates especially when they have possession of the puck. This is essential if they are to give or receive a pass that will include them in the flow of the game.

In very simple terms this means that being too far ahead of your teammate who has the puck is just as inappropriate as being too far behind.

This go in flow drill seems to help players get a feel for synchronized pace or flow. It also helps players to co-ordinate their efforts with the efforts of their teammates.

This is a drill that seems to work best in a half rink area but can probably be utilized on a full rink as well. In teaching this drill I utilize orange cones placed on the sides of the rink as shown in Figure B.4. The pattern of these cones is such that one side will have more cones than the other side. This is to ensure that it will take longer for the players on one side of the rink to skate through the cones than the players on the other side of the rink.

Figure B.4 Go In Flow Drill: Synchronized Player Movement

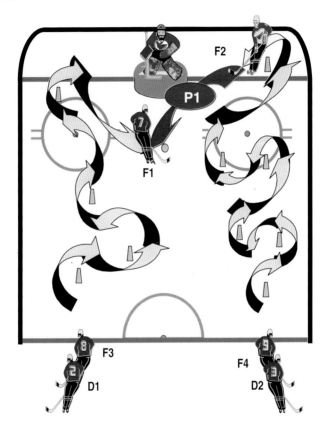

Assemble the players in pairs as linemates one behind the other with one on each side of the rink. As shown in Figure B.4, Red Team forwards F1 and F2 are grouped as linemates, one on each side of the rink as are Red Team forwards F3 and F4, and Red Team defensemen D1 and D2. At first group the players together who normally play together.

On a coach's signal both players begin to skate through the cones on their side of the rink—one with the puck and one without. When the player with the puck has reached and circled his last cone he must pass the puck into the slot area to the other player for an immediate shot on net.

The object of this drill is for both players to reach their final positions at the same time. If one player is a faster skater than the other player is, he must slow down so that he does not get too far ahead of his teammate. The optimum play is for both players to synchronize their movements, slowing down or speeding up as needed, so they are moving in unison with the other.

Once the shot has been released the puck is returned to its starting side and each player skates to the end of the line on the opposite side of the rink to await their next turn.

As shown in Figure B.4, Red Team forward F2 with the puck and Red Team forward F1 have each skated through their cones in synchronized fashion. Red Team forward F2 has completed a pass **[P1]** to the slot area to Red team forward F1 who will now release a shot on net.

Along with the element of synchronized play, this drill allows the players to practice their skating, stickhandling, passing, shooting, and goaltending skills.

As this drill progresses, the players paired together as linemates can be adjusted so that in time each player executes the drill with every other player.

Twisted Wristers Drill

I grew up in a small town in Ontario, Canada in a house with a cinder block basement. For the most part the basement was empty except for a furnace, my mother's washer and dryer, and some laundry tubs. It did not take me long to figure out that this area with its block walls and smooth concrete floor would be a great area to practice shooting hockey pucks. With my father's assistance I was able to paint a life size facsimile of a hockey goal on the wall as a shooting target. My father insisted that I paint a one-foot square in each of the four corners of this net in solid red paint and directed me to aim at these squares. Later a triangle was added at the bottom in the middle to represent the area between the goalie's legs.

After banging ice hockey rubber pucks off this wall area for a few weeks my father became disturbed at the noise created each evening by my pucks hitting the wall with a loud "thump" and rebounding away and hitting the sheet metal furnace covering with a loud "clang".

One evening I went down to my "shooting gallery" to find my pucks altered by my father. The centers in these pucks had been burned out by our furnace poker and replaced by a big glob of lead—a very heavy metal.

Now I could not lift these pucks òff the basement floor. In addition, I could not shoot them with much inertia or speed.

When they did hit the wall they did not make the loud "thump" I was used to hearing and they did not rebound away far enough to make contact with the furnace. Gone was the "clang".

In time as I grew I was finally able to lift these pucks off the floor. Eventually I was able to again make the furnace "clang". On the ice hockey rink my shot improved dramatically and I began to score goals.

Years later I began to understand what my father had done for me. When I began to coach youth roller hockey the memories of my basement shooting gallery led me to construct this drill.

This drill utilizes a "shooter-tutor" to define the shooter's targets. A shooter-tutor can be made from a single sheet of 3/8-inch thick white hard plastic such as high-density polyethylene. The exact dimensions required are 74 inches wide and 48 inches high. It is hung with hooks or tied with ropes from the crossbar of the net. A 12-inch square of material has been removed from each corner of this sheet to represent shooting holes #1 through #4. A similar sized triangle of material has also been removed from the center about 3 inches from the bottom to represent shooting hole #5.

As shown in Figure B.5, the shooter-tutor covers the net and leaves open or uncovered the five shooting holes. These shooting holes are the shooting targets for the players. The object of the drill is for each player in rotation to place a selected number of pucks through each of the five shooting holes. Players should release their shots from a "shooting area" which is 10 to 15 feet out in front of the net in the slot area.

This drill can be run so that all players work on scoring through a single shooting hole before any player can move on to the next shooting hole. The coach should choose the number of pucks required, the spot within the shooting area from which to shoot, and the target hole based on where he thinks each player needs the most practice.

This drill can be run as a competition between players with each player participating in turn. The first player to complete the drill wins. Ties are decided by shootouts with the coach choosing the target hole until a winner emerges.

I have also utilized a variation of this drill as an exercise to build forearm muscle strength and wrist snap speed. Weights can be added to each players stick near the blade for this purpose.

Figure B.5 Twisted Wristers Drill: Using a Shooter-Tutor

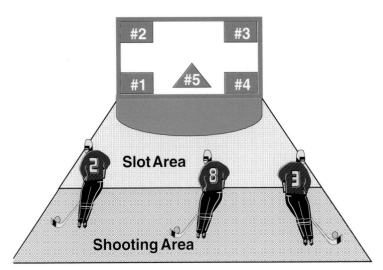

Heavier weighted roller practice pucks are more effective than stick weights but are more difficult to find. I recommend the use of a large heavy 4-inch diameter street hockey puck that I have found to be suitable for an indoor roller hockey rink surface.

These pucks are available in various colors. I am especially fond of the big heavy yellow pucks. I number each puck sequentially using black permanent marker. Each season I assign one of these numbered pucks to each player with written instructions to practice shooting wrist shots with this puck at home.

I have found that a regimen of twice a week shooting practice sessions with a day of rest in between works best. Each session should include no more than 30 shot repetitions. Only forehand and backhand wrist shots should be utilized—slap and snap shots do not provide the rapid muscle development desired.

Players are asked to record and document the date of each session and the total number of practice shots and passes taken on a log. When players begin to see their goal scoring totals increase after a few weeks of home shooting practice sessions, they are motivated to continue.

Once the season has finished, each player is instructed to return the numbered puck assigned to him so that it can be re-assigned to another player during the next playing season. Over the course of each season the use of these pucks has produced encouraging results. Most players have seen dramatic improvement in their ability to release hard and accurate shots on net. As you might expect, the average number of goals scored per game by these players has also risen substantially.

Pass the Eggs Drill

I can still remember the excitement I felt waking up one cold crisp winter morning to find a small ice rink in my own back-yard. While I had been sleeping my dad had taken the garden house and created my own personal ice rink right outside my own back door. It seemed immense to my young eyes—about 20 feet long and about 10 feet wide. I had been playing organized ice hockey for two winters and thought that I was one of the best in my neighborhood. I could hardly wait to lace up my skates and invite my friends over for a game of hockey after school.

But my plans for neighborhood hockey dominance would have to wait. My father put them on hold. On his way out the front door to go to work he told me to stay off the backyard rink after school—to wait until he got home from work that evening—he had something important to show me.

It seemed to take longer than usual for my father to arrive home after work. When he got out of our car he had a large brown paper bag in his arms. I didn't have to wait too long to discover its contents. As we laced up our skates, my dad told me that my skating and shooting skills were progressing nicely but my passing abilities needed a lot of work. My dad went to one end of our backyard rink and I went to the other. We began to pass a puck back and forth between us.

His passes kept hitting my stick and bouncing off to the side or up and over the blade. I remember getting upset that he was passing the puck to me with so much speed that I couldn't keep it on the blade of my stick. His passes would hit my stick and disappear into the snow bank at the edge of the ice surface. After I had dug about a dozen pucks out of the snow, I decided to do to him what he was doing to me. Even though I was returning passes to my father with all the strength and speed I could muster he easily received them and sent them back with as much or more speed.

My father had the knack of receiving my pass on his stick and returning it to me quickly and crisply all in one motion. I watched him carefully trying to figure out how he did this so that I could imitate him. After thirty minutes of digging pucks out of the snow my hands were cold and stiff. I was angry, humiliated, and in tears. My mother, who had been watching from the back bedroom window, finally came outside with steaming mugs of hot chocolate to stop us.

The chocolate warmed us both. I was ready to try again. This time I was more determined than ever to show my dad what I could do. But my dad said it was now time to have some fun.

He opened the bag he had brought home from work and removed a carton of eggs. He removed one of the eggs placed it on the ice in front of the blade of my stick. He said that the puck was like an egg that had to be handled softly so that it would not break.

He rotated the egg lengthwise, placed the end of the egg against the blade of my stick and told me to gently pass it down the ice to him.

I was amazed that the egg did not break as it left the blade of my hockey stick. I could not believe that it did not break when he received it like a puck on the blade of his stick.

During the next few hours I learned how to "catch" a pass softly on the blade of my stick and return it smoothly and crisply all in one motion. My dad had four dozen eggs in that bag. We broke every single one that night. It took a week to scrape all the eggs and their shells up into our garbage can. It took a month for the smell of eggs to disappear from my hockey stick.

When I started to coach inline hockey in Southern California I found that many of my players had "stone hands" just as I did a long time ago. Even though there was an ample supply of eggs in Southern California there were no outdoor backyard rinks like the one my dad had made that cold winter evening in Canada. I would have to find another way to teach this pass catching skill.

I recommend the use of a large, heavy, 4-inch diameter street hockey puck that I have found to be suitable for a roller hockey rink surface. Once I began to use these large heavy pucks in shooting drills, it became clear that their use would also be beneficial in teaching passing skills.

This drill requires the players to assemble in two lines facing each other in pairs about 10 feet apart as shown in Figure B.6.

Each player pair passes the puck back and forth to each other as rapidly as possible. The object is to be able to send a hard crisp pass to your partner that hits the tape on the blade of his hockey stick. He must receive the pass and in one flowing motion return it to his passing partner. The most important aspect of this is continuous motion—the puck and the player's hockey stick should always be moving.

This sounds easy but is not. In order to "catch" the pass each player must develop the habit of bringing his stick back as soon as the puck touches it without having the puck bounce away off or over the blade of his stick. Bringing the stick back with decelerating speed allows the puck direction to be stopped and reversed all in one flowing motion. It is also important to remind each player to look up just before the return pass is released to focus on the target of his return pass—the tape on the blade of his partner's hockey stick.

Figure B.6 Pass the Eggs Drill: Catching the Puck

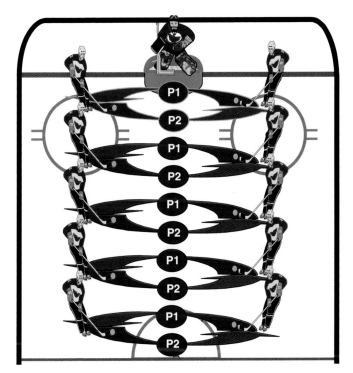

With each successful pass the speed of the return pass should be increased until each pass is harder and more crisply released. After 10 pass iterations each player moves to pair up with a new partner. The end of this drill is achieved when each player pair can execute 10 successful pass iterations with each of his teammates in turn.

The use of the large heavy street hockey pucks helps each player to develop stronger wrist and forearm muscles needed to make hard crisp passes. When receiving passes, the added weight of this puck also assists each player to bring his stick back in order to "catch" the puck on the blade of his stick with a slowing rate of speed.

Over the course of a season I have found each player's ability to send and receive a hard and accurate pass will improve dramatically if this drill is utilized at every practice. I also believe that this drill also aids each player to advance the game puck at all times during game situations. It just seems that the game puck moves on and off each player's stick more quickly than it did at the beginning of each season.

I am very fond of the big, heavy street hockey pucks—especially the yellow colored ones. I number each puck sequentially using black magic marker. Each season I assign one of these numbered pucks to each player with instructions to practice passing with this puck at home as well.

Once the season has finished, each player is instructed to return the numbered puck assigned to him so that it can be re-assigned to another player during the next playing season.

The ability to release and receive a hard accurate pass is an essential skill; along with skating agility and speed, that makes all the others effective. The ability to "catch" a hard crisp pass on the blade of your hockey stick without error is a skill that should be learned first. When players can receive passes consistently they will also be eager to give them to their teammates. When players can receive passes consistently they will be able to release good hard shots on goal. Their role as an effective team player starts with this skill.

Red Rope Drill

When I started to coach roller youth hockey, I found it difficult to convey the concept of shooting angles to my players. Most players had already developed the bad habit of trying to stickhandle past the goal tender every time they got the puck. They would skate in on net as far as they could before they released their shot. As a result the shots were usually weak and along the rink surface. Not surprisingly most goalies at this same age had already discovered that the most effective strategy to block the shot was to stay back in the net and flop down just before the shot was released.

It was difficult to get shooters to "see" the advantages of shooting earlier and from at least 10 feet out in front of the net in the slot area. It was also difficult to get goalies to come out to challenge the shot and, when they did, to get them to "see" the optimum distance they should come out to meet the shooter.

This drill allowed me to solve both these problems. More importantly repetitions of this drill have allowed the players to develop the improved shooting and goaltending skills.

This drill utilizes a 50-foot length of red rope as a visual aid. Attached to each end of this rope is a short loop of bungee cord ending with a hook as shown in Figure B.7.

Figure B.7 The Red Rope

Attach both ends of the red rope to the top of each goal post using the bungee cord and hook. Extend the red rope out into the slot area as far as it will reach to form a triangle as shown below.

With the goalie in the net, the lines made by the red rope define the shooting area or angle available to a puck released at the point of this triangle.

Moving the point of this triangle to different areas in the slot will define the shooting angle from these points.

The lines made by the red rope also will define the maximum distance the goalie should advance out of the net to eliminate the shooter's angle.

As shown in Figure B.8, the Red Team player is releasing his shot from the optimum center position in the slot directly in front of the net. The lines formed by the red rope define the shooting angle available from this point and the distance the goalie needs to advance to eliminate the shooting angle from this point.

Figure B.8 Red Rope Drill: Center Slot Angle

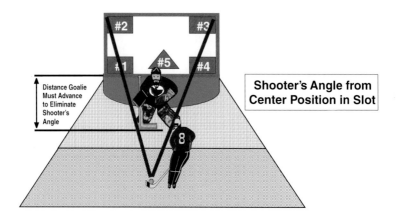

As shown in Figure B.9, the Red Team player is releasing his shot from a position on the left side in the slot area. The lines formed by the red rope define the shooting angle available from this point and the distance the goalie needs to advance to eliminate the shooting angle from this point

Figure B.9 Red Rope Drill: Left Slot Angle

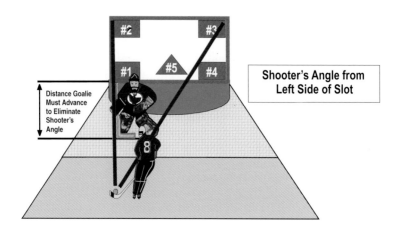

As shown in Figure B.10, the Red Team player is releasing his shot from a position on the right side in the slot area. The lines formed by the red rope define the shooting angle available from this point and the distance the goalie needs to advance to eliminate the shooting angle from this point.

Figure B.10 Red Rope Drill: Right Slot Angle

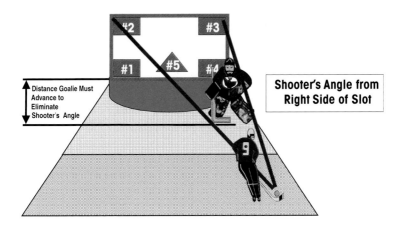

At the start of each season I encourage each individual player to hold the red rope from a number of points within the slot area. Looking down each side of the triangle formed by the red rope, each player is able to clearly "see" the shooting angle he will have from a shot released at each point. I also encourage the goalie to do the same. Looking down each side of the triangle formed by the red rope, the goalie is able to clearly "see" the shooting angle available to the shooter and the distance he must advance in order to eliminate this angle from a shot released at each point.

During the team drill a coach will hold the red rope at chest height from a number of points within the slot area. Players will take pucks from the red line in to the net with the intent of releasing a shot from the point of the triangle. The goalie is encouraged to come out of the net and challenge the shooter by advancing as far as the red rope will allow.

Double Out Drill

This drill requires the players to assemble at the center red line in playing units: one forward line and one defensive line to each unit. As shown in Figure B.11, all players skate either clockwise or counter-clockwise one after the other around the center face-off circle. A coach stands in the middle of this face-off circle with the puck.

Figure B.11 Double Out Drill: Circling the Center

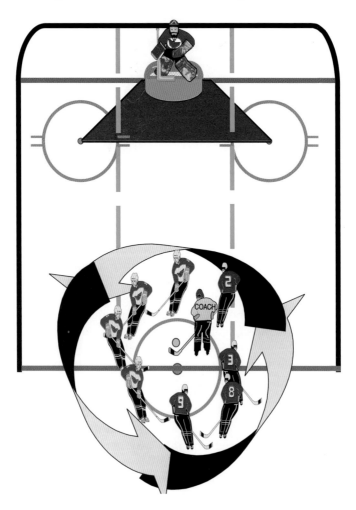

At the coach's discretion he selects a playing unit (usually by calling it's number or practice jersey color) and shoots the puck into one of the corners of the rink. That playing unit then follows the puck into the end zone and executes the double out play while the remaining players continue to skate the center face-off circle.

Figure B.12 Double Out Drill: The Players Roles

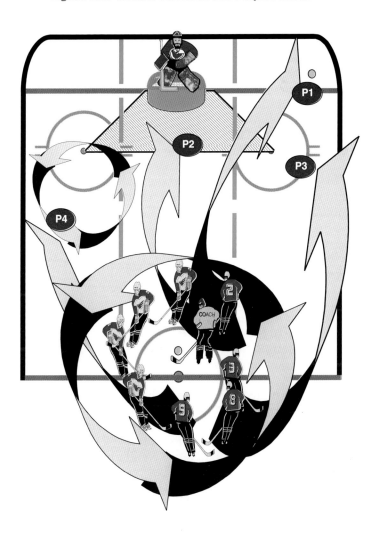

When the puck is advanced over the red line the drill is complete for this playing unit. That playing unit then re-joins the players skating around the face-off circle and the puck is returned to the coach. The drill continues when the coach again selects a playing unit and shoots the puck into one of the corners of the rink.

It is important for the coach running this drill to vary his selection of playing unit and the corner to which he shoots the puck. This gives the players the opportunity to practice a quick turnover of puck possession under simulated game conditions. More importantly it will give players practice playing as a cohesive four-man unit under game conditions.

As shown in Figure B.12, each player's role or responsibility will be depend upon his return into his defensive end. The first player   [**P1**] to return to the defensive end will retrieve the puck. The second player [**P2**] to return to his defensive end go to the front of his net to guard the slot area. The third player [**P3**] will go to the side boards on the same side of the rink as the puck and ready himself to receive the initial breakout pass from the first player who has retrieved the puck. The fourth player [**P4**] to return to the defensive end will circle and fill the other outside lane. Once the initial pass has been made he will accelerate up into the center lane in order to receive the second breakout pass.

Note that each player must immediately react to position of his teammates and assume one of these four responsibilities or roles. His role or responsibility will not be determined by the position he lined up at during the previous face-off.

As shown in Figure B.13, Red Team player #2 was the first man to return to the defensive end and has assumed the responsibility of defenseman D1. He has retrieved the puck and initiated the first double out pass [**P1**] to Red Team player #6. Red Team player #3 was the second man to return into the defensive end and has assumed the responsibilities of defenseman D2. He has gone to the net area to protect the slot. Red Team player #6 was the third man to return into the defensive end and has assumed the responsibilities of forward F1. Red Team player #7 was the last man into the defensive end and has assumed the responsibilities of forward F2. He has received the second [**P2**] breakout pass from Red Team player #6. The remaining players continue to skate counter-clockwise around the faceoff circle awaiting their opportunity to execute this drill.

Figure B.13 Double Out Drill: Breaking Out

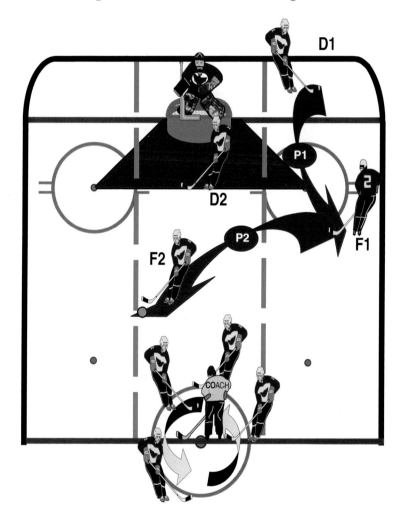

End Zone Chase Drill

This drill is intended to allow players to practice controlling the puck in their opponent's defensive end zone. The main ingredient of this skill is patience. Player's must learn to patiently maintain control of the puck in their opponent's end until a high percentage shot can be released on net.

Figure B.14 End Zone Chase Drill: Maintaining Puck Possession

This drill requires the players to assemble at the red line in playing units: one forward line and one defensive line to each unit. One forward player shoots the puck into one of the corners of the rink. That playing unit then follows the puck into their offensive end zone and gains control of the puck. That playing unit will attempt to maintain control of the puck in the offensive end zone until a high percentage shot can be released on net. One or two forward players act as chasers and follow the puck into the end zone to attempt to recover possession of the puck from the offensive playing unit. When the puck is touched by one of the chasers or is scored on net this drill is over.

itn The puck is brought back to the center red line, shot into one of the corners of the rink, and the next playing unit executes the next drill cycle. Forwards are alternated as chasers on successive drill cycles.

As shown in Figure B.14, the first offensive playing unit has followed the puck into the corner of the end zone. Red Team forwards F3 and F4 with Red Team defensemen D3 and D4 form the second playing unit. Green Team forwards F5 and F6 are the chasers. Red Team forward F1 has gained control of the puck and passed **[P1]** to Red Team defenseman D2. Red Team defenseman D2 has passed **[P2]** to Red Team defenseman D1 and then skated into the high slot area looking for a pass which will allow him to release a high percentage shot on net. Red Team defenseman D1 has passed **[P3]** to Red Team forward F2. Red Team forward F2 has found Red Team defenseman D2 open in the high slot area and passed **[P4]** the puck to him. Red Team defenseman D2 can now release a high percentage shot on net.

The offensive Red Team playing unit has moved the puck to the outside or sideboards in order to spread out the chasers. Spreading out the chasers has made it easier to complete passes around or by them.

This drill emphasizes good passing as well as patience with the puck. The Red Team offensive playing unit has not rushed to release a shot on net. They have completed good perimeter passes and patiently maintained control of the puck until a high percentage shot on net can be released. As long as the puck is not scored or the chasers are not allowed to touch the puck the Red Team playing unit will maintain possession of the puck and this drill will continue.

APPENDIX C

Parent Fan
Stands

Orientation

*T*he material in this APPENDIX is intended to augment the rules and policies documented in writing and distributed by the management of the roller hockey program at your facility. In addition this material should provide general information about the team that your son or daughter will be assigned to this season, the role of the coaches for your son or daughter, and most importantly the role of the parent/fan.

Roller hockey is a great game. Games should always be fun to play. At all age groups in a roller hockey program, roller hockey must always remain just a game that is played for fun. It is recommended that team coaches be dedicated to make the playing season fun for all players, parents, and fans. As a parent/fan it is best that you encourage your son or daughter to remember this fact before and after every scheduled game.

Roller hockey requires specific knowledge and skills. Your team coaches should be dedicated to teach and encourage players to play "smart" roller hockey as they continue to develop their individual physical abilities and natural talents. If they are successful, every player on their team will be able to demonstrate improved roller hockey knowledge and skills by season end. As a parent/fan it is best that you encourage and assist your son or daughter in this endeavor. The more you learn about the game the more you will have in common to discuss and review together.

Roller hockey is a competitive team contest. The character of an individual player is developed and strengthened by winning and losing as a member of a team. It is best if team coaches emphasize team play rather than individual effort. Emphasis should be focused upon:

1. striving to win each game by playing harder and with more effort than any opponent

2. playing smarter roller hockey than any opponent, and

3. playing more unselfishly and more cohesively than any opponent.

As a parent/fan you can best support this approach by refraining from rewarding your son or daughter only for individual efforts. It is recommended that you cheer for every player on either team regardless of his or her ability level.

To do this effectively you should strive to recognize and value every player's contribution to his or her team. You can do this best if you consistently encourage and support all players regardless of the outcome of each scheduled game.

Clear communication is an essential element. If you have any problems or concerns it is best that you talk with your team coaches immediately—give them the first opportunity to address them.

Code of Conduct

*A*ll roller hockey team players should dedicate themselves to a process of continuous learning and advanced skill development over the course of the playing season.

In this educational process players should study educational material containing vital hockey information at home over the course of the season. Your team coaches will generally review the subjects covered in this material with each player during practice sessions.

All players should be expected to comply with their coaches' instruction and requests during practices and games to the best of their abilities.

Parents and players should be encouraged to question their coaches if their instructions are not clearly understood. Open dialog between parents, coaches, and players will promote individual player learning as well as unified team harmony.

Players should show respect for their coaches, for their opponents, for their game officials, and for the game of hockey at all times.

Team coaches should not tolerate equipment throwing, excessive celebrations, complaining about (non) penalty calls, trash-talking, goading, intimidation, or criticism of any player. This is also meant to include excessive displays of anger or temper for any reason such as slapping a hockey stick on the playing surface, against a goal post, or against rink boards and glass.

Players should be positive and encouraging at all times. All players should remember that any form of negative behavior does not help to make any one of them a more proficient hockey player.

Enhanced hockey proficiency can only come from talent, hard work, and dedicated practice infused with constant encouragement and support for *all* players.

Player Equipment

Required Equipment

- **Helmet:** All formal sanctioned roller hockey programs will normally require players to wear an HECC approved helmet with cage straps and chin straps. A full-face shield or cage will generally be required for youth players under the age of 18 years. Full-face shields are strongly recommended for adults as well. Half-face shields are usually required for adults as a minimum.

- **Jersey:** All players will usually be required to wear a regulation team jersey at all games. If a player has forgotten to bring his or her jersey, a jersey can usually be rented from the management of the roller hockey program for a nominal fee.

- **Skates:** All players should utilize suitable in-line hockey skates with no exposed bolts or screws exposed. Generally skates with softer wheels will prevent excessive slipping and falling on the roller hockey rink surface. For a standard Sport Court surface, a 76A or 78A wheel is recommended. All skate brake assemblies should be removed to ensure player safety.

- **Hockey Stick:** All players should utilize a suitable hockey stick. The proper type of hockey stick is required to maximize player skills.

Stick flex or bending ability, similar to a graphite golf shaft, can add speed and power to a shooter's puck. Unfortunately it can also severely diminish shooting accuracy. Until a player has clearly demonstrated his ability to shoot accurately on a consistent basis a stiffer stick shaft might be preferred. This is especially important at starter and lower intermediate levels of play.

Stick length is an important factor. Unfortunately many players utilize a stick that is much too long. A recommended length stick is one that will reach no further than the player's chin when standing on his or her skates.

Most good stickhandlers will utilize a stick having an oversized blade. A larger blade surface helps to manipulate and control the puck. Blades that have been worn down excessively thru street or other use should be removed and replaced. Most good stickhandlers will also tape the entire blade. Tape helps to manipulate and control the puck. Tape softens the blade surface so pucks will have little bounce off the blade surface. Tape also ensures that maximum friction will be maintained between the puck and the stick. Black tape should not be used as it will mark the playing surface—white tape is recommended.

Most good stickhandlers also will play with a stick having a straight or minimum curved blade to improve their stick-handling skills. A stick having a blade that is curved to the maximum allowed might aid the slapshot but it will severely inhibit control of the puck especially when passing or shooting the puck on the backhand side of the stick.

A shorter stick with a straighter, larger blade is best.

● ***Hockey Pads:*** All players should wear roller hockey knee and shin guards, hockey gloves, roller hockey elbow pads, and athletic supporter with hard cup (jock strap).

Goalies should wear a chest protector.

Recommended Additional Equipment

The following equipment is not required but is strongly recommended as well:

1. Roller Hockey Girdle

2. Shoulder and Chest Protector

3. Mouth-guard

4. Pelvic Protector for Female Players

Miscellaneous

All loose jewelry (necklaces, earrings, rings, anklets, or bracelets) should be removed prior to the start of a game or practice. This is essential for player safety.

Playing Time

Recreation Division Programs

In a recreation division hockey program, players are assigned to a specified team by the management of the hockey program. Team coaches generally will have little input into this process except for the reservation of their own sons or daughters to the teams that they themselves coach. In this environment assignments are made with the goal of providing equal or balanced talent on every team.

In these programs a "Balanced Play" rule is normally in effect. This means that every player regardless of ability should play approximately as much as every other player. There is no competition for playing time amongst the players—the least talented should play as much as the most talented.

Unfortunately accurately judging player talent is a very difficult task. As a result some teams will inevitably be assigned a larger number of more talented players than others. It follows that teams that have been assigned the fewest number of the least talented or experienced players will generally be more successful.

In a balanced play environment, teams with one or two very talented players and a larger number of beginner players will not always prevail against a team that has a greater number of mid-level players. The advantage of having very talented players is taken away by the balanced play rule—players with advanced skills can play no more than any other player. Coaching proficiency or experience in this environment is also negated to a great extent by the balanced play rule. The coach can do little except to play each player on his team in turn and to the same extent as any other. As a result in this environment the mid-level players will generally get to play more often against lesser talented starter or beginner players and will usually prevail.

It is best that parents and fans always remember that in a recreation division program, participation and not winning should always be the primary objective.

Within these guidelines, team coaches can be allowed a minimal amount of discretion regarding playing time when level of effort, attitude, and attendance are considered.

Where minimal discretion is allowed, players who regularly attend all scheduled practices, pay attention to their coaches' instructions during scheduled practice sessions, and give their best efforts during scheduled practices should receive a preferential amount of playing time in accordance with balanced play guidelines during scheduled games.

Club Division Programs

In a club division hockey program, team coaches will make all player selections. In this environment selections are made with the goal of assembling a balanced team consisting of the most talented available players.

Unfortunately balance is a very difficult task to accomplish. It is a fact of life that some players will simply have superior skills than others. In addition some players will be more proficient at some skills than other players. Penalty killing, face-offs, and power plays are examples of some of these specialized skills.

In club division programs the coaches can take great advantage of having very talented players on the team. Coaches can attempt to match playing lines against their opponents—putting their most talented players on the rink to negate the skills of the most talented players on the opposition team or to create a skill advantage against an opposition player line that is judged to have lesser capability. Coaching experience and proficiency is of great importance in club division programs.

As a result in club division programs the most talented players will usually play more than lesser talented players. Because balance between competing teams is not being administered by an outside hockey program management staff, there will tend to be a larger number of very talented players on these teams than in a recreation division program. This fosters great competition for playing time amongst the players.

In a club division program, parents and fans should always remember that winning and not participation is the primary objective.

Within these guidelines, team coaches can utilize a great amount of discretion regarding playing time when level of effort, attitude, and attendance are considered.

Players who regularly attend all scheduled practices, pay attention to their coaches' instructions during scheduled practice sessions, and give their best efforts during scheduled practices should receive substantially more playing time during scheduled games.

Shift Length and Line Rotations

Individual player skills are normally severely diminished by fatigue. In addition the chances of injury are significantly increased by fatigue. As a result, the goal should be to have non-fatigued players on the rink at all times. Unfortunately many players never want to volunteer that they are tired enough to get off the rink.

Stoppages in play caused by rule infractions provide an opportunity to change player lines and remove fatigued players. Players having higher skill levels will usually cause fewer rule infractions resulting in longer periods of continuous play. This is not always the case with less skilled players. As a result, playing intervals between these stoppages can be very short or in some cases excessively long.

On-the-fly player line changes also allow fatigued players to be replaced on the rink. In addition, rapid on-the-fly line rotations can help players to remain attentive at all times to the game on the rink. As a direct result, the development of player skills is enhanced when that player can see everything that happens on the rink and can discuss it with coaches and other players as it happens.

In most roller hockey games, there will be very few rule infractions that will cause a stoppage in play. As a result there will be only a few opportunities for rapid player rotation coincidental with a stoppage of play and players should voluntarily rotate their shifts rapidly during the flow of the game.

Players should voluntarily initiate a line change or rotation on-the-fly when they become fatigued or injured. The goal should be to have player shifts that average approximately 1 minute in length with no shifts longer than 90 seconds.

Practice Sessions

General

Practices promote team play and development of advanced skills. Players should be encouraged to attend all practices. Roller hockey is a team sport that requires the coordinated, harmonious effort of all players. It is difficult for players to learn how to play as a coordinated, harmonious unit without repetition and practice.

In general, there should be a minimum of one practice session per week depending upon rink availability.

In most roller hockey programs, participating teams are usually given a number of free half-rink practices that are paid for by player registration fees.

Over the course of the season, most coaches will want to schedule additional practice sessions—some of these will be half-rink sessions, some of these will be full-rink sessions.

Additional Practice Costs

Additional practices will need to be paid for at the current facility rental rates. Because availability of practice time at most facilities can become very limited, additional practices may need to be scheduled at other facilities at even higher rates.

In order to schedule these practices and to cover these costs most coaches should request a nominal practice payment fee from each player. Team coaches will require players to pay for these practices at the beginning of the playing season whether the player plans to attend each practice or not.

If players are not able to comply with this request, it is best to discuss this matter with the team head coach as soon as possible. It is a general practice to return all unused money to parent/fans on a pro-rated equal basis at season end.

Practice Objectives

Practices are for learning. Team coaches should be dedicated each season to assist each player to learn additional hockey skills that will help them to improve their game. When the last game of the season is played his or her improved play should be clearly visible to everyone.

For this reason coaches should request each player to pay close attention to all instructions during practice sessions. The most important aspect of this is "pay attention".
Practices are for conditioning. Team coaches should encourage each player to give their best efforts during practice session drills. Players should also be encouraged to tell their coaches if they are unable to comply because of injury or equipment problems. The most important aspect of this is "best efforts".

Some players, however, may choose not to dedicate themselves to a process of continuous learning and improvement through participation in regular team practices. Team coaches should best view this as a missed opportunity for these players to learn new skills and to practice these new skills through repetition.

Practice Attendance

Regular or consistent attendance at scheduled practices is desired. Players who attend practice regularly will develop advanced skill levels that will allow them to meet the demands of play during scheduled games. Players who attend practices regularly will develop advanced levels of physical conditioning that will better prepare them to meet the demands of play during scheduled games.

Players who attend practices regularly should be rewarded with increased playing time during scheduled games over players who do not attend practices on a regular basis.

Excused Absences

Team coaches need to understand that, from time to time, failure to attend a scheduled practice can be caused by factors that are beyond the control of the player. In these circumstances, players should be formally excused from attendance at scheduled practices by their coaches.

In order to be excused from a scheduled practice, coaches should require one of the player's parents to verbally notify at least one of the player's coaches in advance of the player's absence.

Players who are regularly excused from attending practice sessions may not be selected by their coaches to participate in critical team situations such as penalty defense, power plays or shoot-outs. Because the skill levels of these players may not have been developed to the same extent as their teammates, they will not know how to meet the demands of play required by these special situations during scheduled games. Players who are regularly excused from attending practice sessions will also have poorer physical conditioning than that of their teammates. They are certain to fatigue sooner and increase their chances of injury. To prevent injury it is best if their coaches reduce the length of their playing shifts during scheduled games.

Unexcused Absences

Players, who have not been formally excused from practice attendance, should receive reduced playing time during the next scheduled game.

In a recreation division program, a general rule to follow is to have players who fail to attend a scheduled practice and who's attendance has not been excused in advance by their coaches sit out one full period of play during the next scheduled game for each missed practice.

In a club division program, a general rule to follow is to have players who fail to attend a scheduled practice and who's attendance has not been excused in advance by their coaches sit out one complete game for each missed practice.

In a recreation division program goaltenders are a special case. In a recreation division program goaltenders can only be replaced at the start of each scheduled game and are not permitted to enter a game after sitting out one period. For this reason goaltenders may be forced to sit out the next scheduled game in its entirety for each missed practice that has not been excused in advance by their coaches. When this occurs, the management of the recreation division program will usually provide substitute goaltenders in order to maintain the equality or balance of talent between teams.

In a club division program goaltenders can be replaced with any substitute goaltender on the team roster at any time at the discretion of the coaches just like any other player.

Players who find that they are repeatedly unable to comply with these practice session guidelines or who find them unacceptable should discuss these issues with their coaches.

Team Communications

General

Good team communications are vital to a good roller hockey experience in both the recreation division and club division levels. Good team communications can be facilitated using a variety of written forms as vehicles between coaches, players, and parent/fans. Some recommended examples are described below.

Head Coach Profile

This one page outline should give some information about the background and roller hockey coaching experience of your head coach. This information should provide an introduction that will assist the communication process between players, parent/fans, and the head coach.

Coaches Contact List

This list should provide names, telephone contact numbers and email addresses for all team coaches. This information allows players and parent/fans to quickly contact any coach as required to verify player attendance at scheduled games and practices or to discuss player status and development progress.

Player Roster

Prior to the first scheduled game it is recommended that team coaches provide each player and parent/fan with a comprehensive listing of all players for the current season. Each player should be identified by name and jersey number along with the first names of parents and a home telephone number. This information can be useful in arranging joint rides to and from rink facilities.

Player Email List

Another excellent vehicle that promotes team communications is email. Today nearly every player and parent/fan has this capability already in place and is familiar with its use. Providing a listing of current email addresses for all players is strongly recommended. This information should assist the communication process between players, parent/fans, and team coaches by encouraging and facilitating email contact among all team participants.

Team Statistics

It is recommended that team statistics be recorded on a game by game basis. Statistics should include goals scored for, goals scored against, shots on goal attempted, goaltender saves, scoring percentage, goaltender save percentage, goals per game average, and goals against average. Statistics such as these should assist coaches to determine which individual player skills require additional development efforts during practices. These statistics will also indicate which team skills will require additional development.

Game Schedule

At the beginning of each playing season, it is appropriate to provide a complete schedule of games for coaches, players and parent/fans. This schedule should include game dates, start times, playing locations, and home and visitor team assignments. In some cases player snack responsibilities can also be listed. In this way everyone will be informed, and can communicate or resolve any scheduling conflicts.

Practice Schedule

At the beginning of each playing season, it is advisable to provide a complete schedule of practices to coaches, players and parent/fans. This schedule should contain practice dates, start times, and practice locations. Both currently scheduled and as yet unscheduled or intended practices should be identified so that everyone will be informed. In this way conflicts as well as potential schedule conflicts can be identified and resolved.

Game Lineup

Prior to each scheduled game, each player or parent/fan in attendance should be provided with a game lineup for that scheduled game. Each active player should be identified by name and jersey number. In addition, initial forward and defensive line assignments should be listed for the current game. It is also recommended to include a game scoring summary section as part of this lineup form. This summary should provide parent/fans watching in the stands with columns to list the period number, the clock time, player jersey number and initials for each goal scored, as well as the player number and initials for all assists.

Game lineups in this format will aid family members watching in the stands to quickly identify each player by jersey number and name during the course of each game. This should promote discussion among parent/fans watching in the stands during the course of the game. In most cases, after the first few scheduled games, parent/fans will naturally sit together as a group and cheer together as a group during the course of the game. This of course promotes great team harmony.

Game lineups may also include a schedule of the next few games and practices as a quick reminder of the most current upcoming team events.

Team News Bulletin

From time to time it will be necessary to communicate late breaking changes to scheduled games or practices as well as notification of new unscheduled events and meetings. It is recommended to document and distribute these in the form of a team news bulletin from the team coaches. In this way everyone will be immediately informed, and will be able to communicate or resolve any scheduling conflicts.

Player Profile

At the start of each playing season it is recommended to ask each player to complete and submit a player profile questionnaire form. This questionnaire should be designed to provide the team coaches with some hockey history about each player as well as a statement of the goals each player and parent/fan would like to accomplish during the current hockey season.

Goals should be defined to be what each player and parent/ fan wants to learn, improve, or accomplish during this season. These are the things that team coaches should help each player with during this season. Specifying these goals in writing helps each player and parent/fan to agree and to focus on what is really important to him or her. Completing this questionnaire conveys a commitment to learn and practice them. Completing this questionnaire communicates these goals clearly to the team coaches.

Team Meeting Notice

It is recommended that one or more formal team meetings be held during the course of the season. All players, their parents, and their family members should be invited and are expected to attend. These meetings can take many forms but are usually most effective if they are held away from the rink facility in a non-game or practice environment. Pizza parties, picnics, lunches, barbeque parties, and pool parties are some of the usual favorite formats. Team coaches should be prepared to discuss current team progress and status with parent/fans and players at this meeting. Two-way feedback in this type of setting promotes and enhances team harmony.

Sample Forms

Player Roster

Player Name	Jersey#	Position D/F/G	Birthdate mm/dd/yy	Mother/Dad Name	Contact Telephone

Position: D = Defenseman F = Forward G = Goaltender

Player Email List

Player Name	Email Address

Email Address: name@ispname.com/net/org

Parent Fan Stands

Player Profile

Player Information	
Team Name:	
Player Name:	Jersey #:
Player Age:	Date of Birth (mm/dd/yy):

Player Profile			
Previous Number of Seasons Played:			
Preferred Position (Check One)	Foward	Defense	Goaltender
Shot Type (Check One)		Left	Right

Goals For This Season
Player Goals:
Parent Goals:

Please Return to Your Head Coach at Your Next Practice

123

Game Schedule

Date	Day of Week	Start Time	Team Names Visitor @ Home	Snacks: Player Name	Game Result

Game Result: W = Win or L = Lose Followed by Score
e.g. W 7–5

Practice Schedule

Practice Date	Day of Week	Practice Start Time	Practice #	Practice Location

Game Lineup

	Player Name	#	Player Name	#
Goaltenders:				
Defense:				
Offense:				
Absent:				
Inactive:				

Scoring Summary	Period #	Clock Time	Goal Scored By	Assist #1 By	Assist #2 By
Enter: Period #, Clock Time, Player #, Player Initials For Each Goal Scored					

Current Schedule
Please Notify One Of Your Coaches **If You Cannot Attend A Practice Or Game!**

Player Statistics

GAME #		1		2		3		3		5		6		7		8		9		10		Total	
Player Name	#	G	A	G	A	G	A	G	A	G	A	G	A	G	A	G	A	G	A	G	A	G	A
TOTALS:																								

Team Statistics

OFFENSE	1	2	3	4	5	6	7	8	9	10	Total
Shots Taken											
Goals Scored											
Scoring %											
Cumulative Shots Taken											
Cumulative Goals Scored											
Goals Scored Per Game Average											

DEFENSE	1	2	3	4	5	6	7	8	9	10	Total
Shots Against											
Goals Against											
Saves Against											
Save %											
Cumulative Shots Against											
Cumulative Goals Against											
Cumulative Saves Against											
Goals Against Per Game Average											

ENGINEERED

OVERALL HIGHER SHOT
VELOCITY DESIGN

FLOATING GLIDE PIN MOVES UP
AND DOWN TO ABSORB
VIBRATION ALLOWING THE
PUCK TO FLATTEN OUT FASTER

CUSTOM SIDE TEXTURING FOR
BETTER STICK/PUCK TRACTION
RESULTING IN INCREASED PUCK
CONTROL AND SHOT ACCURACY

45° ANTI-FLIP
RELIEF DESIGN

BUILT-IN IMPACT
ABSORBING WINDOWS
FOR LESS REBOUND

PVC BODY WITH
BUILT-IN SHOCK
PIN SYSTEM

THE PUCK COMPANY
ROLLER
SHOCK™
U.S.A.
HOCKEY
MADE IN USA

PATENTS PENDING

WWW.SHOCKHOCKEY.COM

Order Form

To order any of the books listed below, you can write to us directly, contact your local book store, FAX, or order online at: www.GabrielBooks.com

Roller Hockey: The Game Within the Game, by Warren Taylor $19.95
An in-depth guide to this growing sport. Ideal for coaches, players and fans.

Books for Financial and Business Growth:

Couples and Money, by Victoria Collins, PhD $13.95
A vital guide for couples to thrive financially and emotionally. It provides exercises and instructions for couples to talk about money. Recommended by Consumer Credit Counseling Service.

Wealth On Any Income, by Rennie Gabriel,
   CLU, CFP (UCLA Instructor) $17.95
Move from creating financial goals to achieving them. Covers both the emotional and practical aspects of handling money effectively. Endorsed by Mark Victor Hansen, co-author of the *Chicken Soup for the Soul*® series.

Wealth On Any Income cassette tape program $59.00
Five hours read by Rennie Gabriel from his book. It is a comprehensive, but simple to use, program for anyone to handle money effectively, get out of debt, live within their income, start investing with as little as $100 and ultimately create financial independence. Includes the full book and two spending registers.

How to Outwit and Outsell Your Competition, by Shirley Lee $14.95
Grow your business 50-200% per year using little known, powerful strategies that cannot fail. Avoid costly marketing blunders by learning the common mistakes.

The REALTOR® Series:

Our REALTOR® series of books will show you how to get the best deal when buying a home. They are currently available for the states listed below and are all $17.95 each.

For additional information, please call (800) 940-2622.

How to Make Your REALTOR® Get You the Best Deal,

> **Colorado 2ⁿᵈ Edition**
> **Idaho Edition**
> **Indiana Edition**
> **Illinois Edition**

Kansas Edition

Louisiana Edition

Michigan Edition

Minnesota Edition

Montana Edition

Nevada Edition

New York Edition

Oklahoma Edition

Southern California Edition

Texas Edition

Washington Edition

Order Form–Please Copy, Fill Out, Mail, Fax, Phone or Go Online

Name_____

Address_____

City, State, zip_____

Daytime phone (____)_____

e-mail address_____

Product Description	Quantity	Total
_____	_____	$_____
_____	_____	$_____
_____	_____	$_____
_____	_____	$_____

Sales tax, (only for orders delivered in CA) 8% $_____

Shipping and handling, $4 per book or tape $_____

Total: $_____

❏ check enclosed $_____

❏ please charge my M/C or Visa #_____

Expiration date_____

Signature as on the card_____

Mail to: Gabriel Publications
14340 Addison Street #101
Sherman Oaks, CA 91423-1832
or fax to (818) 990-8631
www.GabrielBooks.com

Additional Offers

On-Line Orders: Orders for additional copies of this book can be submitted on-line. Multiple copies of this book for team distribution can also be ordered on-line. Substantial discounts are available for larger quantities ordered. Please access the General Store Books & Manuals section in web site: http//www.rollerhockeycoach.com.

Free Coaches Forms: The author and publisher have generously agreed to provide copies of forms appearing at the end of this book at no charge. These forms can be downloaded to you by accessing the General Store Free Coaches Forms section in web site: http://www.rollerhockeycoach.com or by sending an email request to the author at: warrentaylor@roller hockeycoach.com. All other material is for use by permission only.

Player Exam Forms: Player examination forms have been created to allow each player and coach to verify that the instruction material found in Chapters 2 through 11 of this book has been read and learned. These examinations consist of a series of multiple choice questions covering each major subject. Examinations and their corresponding answer sheets can be ordered and downloaded to you by accessing the General Store Player Exam Forms section in web site: http://www.roller hockeycoach.com.

On-Line Learning System: Access to an on-line review and examination facility is also available. Prior to completing a selected examination, the player/student can review the selected chapter material on his computer screen, then submit his answers on-line. The selected examination will be graded immediately and the results displayed on-line. This provides relevant and immediate feedback to each player/student. This enhanced learning system will create and store a player/student record for each examination completed. Players, parents, and coaches can review the current accumulated examination history for each player/student by accessing an on-line player/student education report summary. Access to the on-line learning system can be ordered and made available by accessing the

General Store On-Line Learning System section in web site: http://www.rollerhockeycoach.com.

Coach Clinics: One of our expert coaches will come to your rink facility to help you develop your coaching techniques and knowledge. A nominal fee will be charged for each scheduled clinic. All required travel/per diem will be charged at actual cost incurred.

Coach clinics can be requested and scheduled by accessing the General Store Coach Clinics section in web site: http://www.rollerhockeycoach.com.

Team Tune-Ups: One of our expert coaches will come to your team practice to help you "tune-up" your team for advanced play. An hourly fee will be charged for each scheduled team session. All required travel/per diem will be charged at actual cost incurred. Team tune-ups can be requested and scheduled by accessing the General Store Team Tune-Ups section in web site: http://www.rollerhockeycoach.com